GET SMARTER MARKETING

Praise for *Get Smarter Marketing*

"Jill Brennan has written a very smart book, aptly titled Get Smarter Marketing. Clearly targeted at small business owners, Jill really shows her expertise and deep understanding of the challenges facing small business owners in a rapidly evolving world. She identifies the pain points as well as the opportunities and puts it all in a way that makes great sense. Any small business owner who reads Get Smarter Marketing and follows Jill's wonderful advice will end up with a marketing plan that I think will have a profound impact on the profitability of their business. I highly recommend this book."

—**Andrew Griffiths**, International business author,
12 books sold in over 60 countries.

"Working with Jill taught me that, in 2015, the use of effective marketing in small businesses is more critical than ever. A well thought out, clearly defined and prioritized marketing plan will provide a vital road map for your business. It will also ensure you get the very best value for your marketing spend."

—**Don Blair**, Founder of the Litmus Group

"From the outset, Get Smarter Marketing clearly provides the vision to develop a marketing plan for small business. Jill Brennan has crafted this book for businesses that know what they want just not sure how to get there. This book divulges not only the how but also the why to planning the strategy for sound business development. Every business owner should read this book—there are practical gems for all."

—**Rodney Young**, Managing Director, Masters and Young Pty Ltd

"Get Smarter Marketing is an essential read for businesses that want to grow yet most likely don't know where to start with marketing. It is packed with clear and practical ways for businesses to get going, and lots of case studies to make everything relevant. All the foundations of good marketing are here, as well as the latest marketing tools that will definitely make a difference to the growth of your business."

—**Amanda Bigelow**, Health Coach

GET
SMARTER
MARKETING

THE SMALL BUSINESS
OWNER'S GUIDE
TO BUILDING A SAVVY BUSINESS

JILL BRENNAN

NEW YORK

NASHVILLE • MELBOURNE • VANCOUVER

GET SMARTER MARKETING
THE SMALL BUSINESS OWNER'S GUIDE
TO BUILDING A SAVVY BUSINESS

© 2018 JILL BRENNAN

Published in New York, New York, by Morgan James Publishing. Morgan James is a trademark of Morgan James, LLC. www.MorganJamesPublishing.com

The Morgan James Speakers Group can bring authors to your live event. For more information or to book an event visit The Morgan James Speakers Group at www.TheMorganJamesSpeakersGroup.com.

ISBN 978-1-68350-392-7 paperback
ISBN 978-1-68350-393-4 eBook
Library of Congress Control Number: 2016921240

Edited by:
Jacqueline Pretty

Cover Design by:
Katrina Tan
and Rachel Lopez
www.r2cdesign.com

Interior Design by:
Bonnie Bushman
The Whole Caboodle Graphic Design

In an effort to support local communities, raise awareness and funds, Morgan James Publishing donates a percentage of all book sales for the life of each book to Habitat for Humanity Peninsula and Greater Williamsburg.

Get involved today! Visit
www.MorganJamesBuilds.com

"Small business isn't for the faint of heart. It's for the brave, the patient and the persistent. It's for the overcomer."
Anonymous

To all ambitious small business owners who have the courage to make their own way and do what others can't or won't.

CONTENTS

INTRODUCTION

Getting noticed in a world that has gone brand crazy is hard. It's estimated that the average person sees between 3,000 and 20,000 brands each day. From the labels you see when you open the pantry doors to a trip to the mailbox overflowing with junk mail and through the onslaught that peppers the daily commute; brands are everywhere.

On top of this, many big brands are backed by dizzying marketing budgets to make sure they are first ones that come to mind for consumers looking for specific solutions.

According to Adweek, Coke's advertising budget was $3.3 billion in 2013 and Matt Powell, a sports industry analyst, put Nike's spending on 'demand creation' in 2014 at just over $3 billion. When you break it down—"that's $8 million per day, $350,000 per hour, $6,000 per minute, $100 per second"—that number is even more astounding.

In Australia, Hall of Fame Business Solutions identified the top advertiser in 2013 as Wesfarmers with a budget of $237.2 million, followed by Woolworths with $176.9 million spend on media advertising.

Advertising in mainstream media is priced for these bigger companies. If you want to run a large billboard advertisement in one prominent location in Melbourne you can expect to pay around $30,000 plus printing and installation. If you want to take out a full-page ad in the Sydney Morning Herald then it will cost around $70,000 plus design costs.

Mainstream media advertising requires deep pockets and an ongoing commitment to have an impact.

This means small businesses can no longer hope that their audience will find them. Nor can they sporadically try different marketing techniques and platforms in the hope that something might stick.

So how do small businesses with limited budgets and resources stand out in a sea of logos?

They need to know how best to reach their target audience. This book will teach you how.

ANOTHER MARKETING BOOK?

First, let's talk about the elephant in the bookshop. Does the world need yet another marketing book? Really? I thought hard about that before beginning and I believe that the answer is yes, it does.

If you've taken a look at the business section in a bookstore or searched online for marketing publications then you know there is no shortage of titles available. And that is just in the small business marketing space. When you look at the overall number of marketing and sales texts, then the number swells exponentially.

So what makes this book different from every other business marketing book?

This book specifically targets the owners of ambitious small businesses that are stuck in a turnover rut and want to take control of their growth. In my work as a marketing consultant, mentor and business owner working with small businesses I see that they typically experience three main problems:

- Marketing can be confusing and without a plan, often a haphazard approach is used.
- Without knowing what is possible with marketing and having the right skills and expertise it can be difficult to implement marketing activities.
- Many businesses are stuck doing the same thing, getting the same results and don't know how to effectively communicate so that customers understand who they are and what problems they can help solve.

This book addresses these problems and provides simple, practical and step-by-step advice for business owners on how to connect with customers, share their products with more people and ultimately achieve profitable growth.

How? By teaching you to create a marketing plan.

YOUR MARKETING PLAN

Most people know that planning, like flossing, is important but often it doesn't happen as frequently as it needs to. If you're in this position, it's probably due to two reasons. Firstly, you are too busy running the business to have time to pull back and strategize. Secondly, the idea of marketing feels completely overwhelming and not knowing where to start means you don't start at all.

However, not having a strategy is like heading out in the car in a new city without a map of where you want to go.

You may get there eventually but you won't be taking the quickest or easiest route. You may even get lost.

Instead you want a plan that will draw in new customers, encourage repeat business, create raving fans and spread word of mouth buzz. In other words, you want a plan that you can use to grow your business.

THE KEY ELEMENTS OF YOUR MARKETING PLAN

If you enter 'marketing plan template' into a search engine you'll find so many different options it can quickly become overwhelming.

There are many different components that you could have in a marketing plan and if you run a larger business it would be expected that you would go all out on most of them. But for smaller businesses that want to see results without a lot of fluff, I've narrowed it down to the following key parts:

Situational analysis

The first piece of any marketing strategy is having a clear understanding of where you are and what you want to achieve. While many small businesses have a strong understanding of their competition and their market, what they are often less familiar with is detailed analysis of their own operations. This can range from things like where their website traffic comes from and what their conversion rate is, through to having a clear brand identity.

In Chapters 1 and 2 I'll help you get clear on who you are and how you want to be perceived in the market place, from having a strong 'why' to developing your brand identity.

Your target market

Once you are clear on who you are and how you want to be represented, the next step is choosing your target market. The big mistake many small businesses make is trying to market to everyone, but this leads to you sending vague or fuzzy messages into the world that don't really connect with anyone, and wasting a lot of time and money marketing on platforms that don't bring benefits to your business.

Instead, you need to focus on a single group, or niche, of customers. Then you can target your marketing directly to them and present your products in the right places, which will lead to a higher return on your marketing investment. Chapter 3 will show you how.

Marketing collateral

The next step is creating collateral—what marketing material do you need to reach that market? This might include your website, brochures, videos, audio material and interactive resources, all of which will be defined by your brand identity and what your target market wants. In Chapter 4 you'll discover my tips and tricks for developing that collateral efficiently and effectively.

Reaching your target market

Once you have collateral, the next step is to consider how it will reach your target market. Which marketing platforms will you use? Different platforms are more effective for different businesses and markets. In Chapter 5 you'll learn about your options and the pros and cons of each, while Chapter 6 will help you choose the right marketing platforms for your business.

Keeping track

After you start marketing across various platforms, it's important to measure your results. This means you can determine the most effective platforms and strategies for your business, as well as improve performance across the board. In Chapter 7 you'll discover the key metrics you'll need to measure, while Chapter 8 will give you ideas for optimizing your marketing efforts.

PUTTING YOUR PLAN TO WORK

Part 1 of this book focuses on the strategic steps required to get your marketing off the ground, or to develop your existing marketing efforts. However, once you've got your marketing plan worked out the question becomes, how can you make the plan happen?

In Chapter 9 I'll share different processes and tools you can use to make your marketing repeatable and scalable, while Chapters 10 and 11 will discuss the different ways you can source marketing help, including hiring internal staff, outsourcing, and the key questions to ask to find the right person or team.

Once you finish, this book will give you the confidence to make informed choices in respect to marketing your business and growing your sales.

The aim of this book is not to turn you into a marketing manager. You will not know every single thing about marketing after reading this (and I'm sure you don't want to know it—you'd rather focus on the rest of your business). You will, however, be armed with the key steps and concepts that will give you a big-picture view of what marketing can do for your business. By the end of this book, you'll know enough to be able to hold your own with marketers and ask the right questions if you need more information.

HOW CAN I BE SO SURE?

I first started working with small businesses over twenty years ago, helping local Australian companies to set up trading and partnership arrangements with companies in Japan.

After doing this for a number of years, I decided to take a leap into the unknown and set up my own business. I created an innovative online membership service that was at the forefront of the shift towards digital services. The learning curve around running a small business was steep, as was becoming adept at the new world of online marketing.

While the business did gain some traction among the target market, not enough people were prepared to pay to make it viable so I decided to change direction.

From that painful (and expensive) experience, I learned many valuable lessons. One of the key lessons was the importance of finding out what people want and giving it to them. Ideas are great, but without testing there is no telling whether your target market will actually buy your product when you embark on a full launch. The market is the great arbiter and there's no point in railing against it and whether you think it's fair or not. If I'd spent some more time up front validating my assumptions about what the market wanted, this could have saved me a lot of frustration and would likely have led me to set up a very different offering.

This experience led to a broader interest in what it takes to motivate customers to take action. Instead of creating my own products, I began promoting other companies' products and services as an affiliate. This involved buying advertising to promote specific offers and receiving commissions on the conversion of each new sale or lead. I did this for a number of years and was able to generate thousands of leads and sales in very competitive niches like dating, finance, insurance, retail, training, licensed gaming and health services. Being an affiliate and operating on the often very thin margin between costs and revenue was useful in honing my understanding of lead generation and minimizing risk to maximize profit.

In the last seven years, I have run my own consulting business and have worked with a number of small businesses to help them find the best path to market their products and services and increase sales.

With this book, which covers every aspect of the marketing process from refining your marketing message to getting repeat business, you will be able to do the same in your business.

PART 1
YOUR MARKETING PLAN

CHAPTER 1

FIND YOUR
'BIG PICTURE'

C ustomers today have more choices than ever before, so simply talking about the features and benefits of your solution isn't enough to make you stand out. Instead, most customers want to be part of something bigger than themselves. This is why people donate to charity. It's why they take on feats of human endurance like running a 100km ultra marathon in the middle of summer and raising money for homelessness at the same time. They want to motivate themselves to achieve something they didn't think they could and to do it in a way that prompts others to support them and the cause they are championing.

Most people want to have a positive impact on the world around them, and one of the ways they can make that contribution or that impact is through the money they spend on products and services. For example, if a family is going to spend money on hot water, why not buy a solar hot water system that uses less energy and is better for the environment than an electric system?

Being clear on why you do what you do, where you want to go and how you want to get there gives your customers the opportunity to have that positive impact and to be a part of something bigger. If customers believe in what you believe and what you want to achieve, they feel good about supporting you. This builds trust that not only makes them more likely to buy from you but will also make them want to share your products with others.

Meanwhile, understanding why you do what you do, what you want to achieve and how you will do it as a business owner will make you think differently about your business. You'll be motivated to think more strategically about your business, to lift your eyes beyond the day-to-day and seek out tools, strategies and expertise that reinforce your reason for being in business and help you achieve your goals.

So how do you achieve this clarity, draw in more customers and set your business apart? You need to define your beliefs, your vision and your values.

START WITH WHY

As Simon Sinek argues in his book Start with Why, 'people don't buy WHAT you do, they buy WHY you do it.' Customers are drawn to businesses that have a greater purpose than simply making money because it means the money they spend makes them feel good about their choices and themselves.

From your perspective, a funny thing happens when you discover your 'why'. If it is truly what drives you then it becomes an inspiring call to action with a motivating force of its own and drives everything that you and your team do.

As a small business owner I doubt your reason for being in business is to simply make money. After all, you could be making money in a job that doesn't come with all of the complications and stresses of a small business. So what's your 'why'? What's the passion behind your business? When trying to work out what motivates you, it may be necessary to brainstorm some key phrases and see how they sit in the context of your life. Your 'why' is very likely to be hiding in plain sight, as your life probably already reflects what you value; you just haven't thought of it in that way. The things you surround yourself with, the activities you choose to do, what you're most proud of, how you spend your time and your money and the issues that get you fired up all make up what drives you.

Grab a sheet of paper and write down your top three priorities for each of the following to point you in the right direction.

- What drives you?
- What gets you out of bed in the morning?
- What makes you feel energized?
- What do you believe in?
- What do you value most?
- What do you surround yourself with?
- What hobbies do you most enjoy?
- What are you most proud of?
- How do you spend your time?
- How do you spend your money?
- What issues get you fired up?

If these questions aren't enough to give you clarity, then you may need to delve into this exercise more deeply. If so, John Demartini's book The Values Factor is an excellent place to start and features many practical exercises that will help you more fully explore this area.

It can also help to see what this looks like for other companies. Sometimes it can be hard to spot as companies don't always have a direct answer to the question 'why do you do what you do?' Instead it is usually the part of a sentence that follows 'believe' or 'passion' on the 'about us' or 'company' page of a website or brochure.

Let's take Lululemon, for example. Lululemon is an active wear brand. What drives this business? They believe in sweating every day.

Collective Magazine is about challenging the status quo, which is demonstrated by their tag line—'game changers | thought leaders | rule breakers | style makers'.

Meanwhile, Totokaelo is a fashion retailer that is trying to stand out through the careful curation of products it sells. 'We believe the art and objects a person chooses for their life are a reflection of values and perspective. We hope to provide a unique point of view that attracts those of similar mind.'

All of the examples above provide a reason for operating that underpins the type of business they are in and provides a platform from which all product and business decisions are made.

HOW TO EXPLAIN YOUR 'WHY'

The key to creating a compelling 'why' isn't just about working out what it is, but wording it in a way that others can embrace too. This doesn't need to be a long, rambling fireside chat about the meaning of life. While it may start out that way, you will then need to distil your 'why' to a sentence or two.

Some examples:

Backroads is a company that runs walking, hiking and biking tours. On their website the owner and founder, Tom Hales, states that he believes 'the world is best experienced up close and under one's own power'.

Elon Musk, a former owner of PayPal and the entrepreneur behind Tesla Motors, the creator of mass-market electric cars, wants to radically change the world for the better.

Google's 'why' is the democratization of information, to make as much information as possible accessible to everyone.

My 'why' is to empower others to innovate beyond what they thought was possible and create a far better tomorrow than they imagined today.

Once you've figured out what the motivating force is that drives you, the next step is to work out what you want to do with that information. How will you use it to shape the future direction of your business? This is done by crafting your vision.

THE VISION TO ACHIEVE YOUR 'WHY'

Your vision is the over-arching long-term goal for your business. If your 'why' is the reason behind your business, your vision is what you are going to achieve, or the impact you want to have on the world.

A clear vision gives your customers a common goal that they can support with their time, energy and money, which contributes to making them feel like they are a part of something significant.

For employees, having a common goal acts as a unifying force. Employees can better articulate what your business is about to both your customers and anyone who asks them what they do and where they work. Working for a small business doesn't always have the allure that comes with a big corporate, but they can be the envy of their friends if they are working for a company that is trying to achieve a larger goal.

For you, a clear vision is one of the keys to being seen as a leader—in your business and in the wider market place. Successful leaders inspire others to follow them. They make others want to join them on their journey, because that journey enhances their own life. In order to inspire others to enlist on your journey, you need to know where you are going.

Aligning your 'why' with a vision for the future is a great combination, as your vision is your 'why' in action. It's how you achieve your reason for being.

Take a moment to ask yourself, where do you want to take your 'why'? What sort of impact do you want to have? How can you bring your passion to life? What will that look like?

If you look at the visions for some of the companies I mentioned earlier, you can clearly see this connection. Backroads' vision is to be 'The World's No1 Active Travel Company'. Google's vision is 'to organize the world's information and make it universally accessible and useful.' Tesla Motors' vision is to 'accelerate the world's transition to sustainable transport'.

My vision is to help small businesses develop the systems and processes of big business while maintaining the dynamism and flexibility that comes from being small and nimble so they can solve tomorrow's problems.

To work out your vision, ask yourself:

- If you could achieve anything, what would it be?
- What would make you sit back and go 'wow, it would be amazing if I could do that'?
- What would have an impact beyond your current business?

THE VALUES GUIDING YOUR VISION

The next step in realizing your 'why' and your vision is to determine your values. Your values are your guiding principles. If your vision is the destination on your journey, your values define how you get there. For example, is it about winning at any cost or do you want to create a family atmosphere among your employees so they enjoy coming to work each day?

Values that Backroads have woven into their business model are quality, trust and being active. Google has a list of ten guiding principles on their website that outline the type of service they offer, including democracy, 'fast is better than slow' and 'you can make money without doing evil'. According to Tesla's website, their principle value is, 'We do not compromise on innovation, performance, or design.' They also value agility, efficiency and excellence.

My values for achieving my vision for small businesses are integrity, innovation and practicality.

To work out your vision, consider the following questions:

- What principles currently guide your business?
- What qualities do you want to be known for by your customers, suppliers and employees?
- What words do you want people to use when they describe your business?

Keep in mind that, for your values to have a real impact, they need to be evident in the way you operate. While customers are understandably skeptical of companies throwing around over-used words like 'quality' and 'honesty', if these attributes are woven into the way you do business then they can experience them and don't need to just rely on what you say. Values in action are far more powerful than words on a page.

PUTTING IT ALL TOGETHER

All these three elements together—Beliefs, Vision, Values— form the core-operating platform for your business and define how decisions are made and opportunities assessed. This makes them a powerful combination that will largely remain the same over the long-term.

Consider the example of Eric Orton to see how beliefs, vision and values work together to help define your marketing strategy. Eric Orton is a running coach and was featured in the bestselling book *Born to Run* by Christopher McDougall. His 'why' is to help people to become better runners so they can move beyond fear and limitations. He sees running as a conduit to emotional and physical empowerment.

In order to realize this and have a bigger impact, he set a vision of one runner per household throughout the world.

This has led to him writing a book *The Cool Impossible* which explains how to improve as a runner from the perspective of running technique as well as mental attitude and diet.

His values include respect for nature and experiencing life to the fullest. In order to comply with those values and not just make money through book sales, he produced a range of training tools to help with running skill development and shoes that reflect his minimalist training style.

To ensure that learning didn't just stop once people got a copy of the book, he also set up a forum where those interested in his methods could interact with each other and he runs several running camps each year in the mountains of Wyoming.

If his vision wasn't to have a runner in each household then he wouldn't have been as motivated or focused on spreading his message beyond his local area. He could have continued to work one-on-one with the athletes and small groups of athletes who were interested in working with him. He wouldn't need to create tools and products that are easy to access no matter where you live.

In other words, his beliefs, vision and values aren't just words on a page—they have influenced the direction of his business as a whole.

SUMMARY

Many small businesses, especially those that have been operating for a while, don't review why they do what they do, how they do it or their big-picture goals. However, there is power in articulating your beliefs, your vision and how you want to get there that has flow-on benefits for your marketing, your customers and your business.

KEY ACTIONS

❖ To figure out what drives you, get a piece of paper and write down your top three priorities for each of the 'why' questions. See if there are any recurring themes in your answers.

❖ Create a 'why' statement that sums up your answers and sit with it for a couple of days.

❖ Once you've worked out your 'why', answer the vision questions. What do you want to achieve?

❖ Finally think about which guiding principles will take you there.

❖ Put all three elements into one document so that you can easily view each one and share them with others.

❖ Sit with it for a week and see if it needs any tweaking. Once you're happy with the outcome, begin sharing it with others—friends, family, employees and, finally, customers.

CHAPTER 2

DEVELOP YOUR BUSINESS IDENTITY

T he mistake most small businesses make when they start marketing is to jump right in. They create a website, get some brochures designed, dabble in different forms of advertising and then wonder why they don't get results. The issue is usually that they didn't do enough work up front.

Instead of diving straight in to designing marketing collateral, in this chapter we're going to take a look at your brand, your business story and your product story.

DEFINE YOUR BRAND

What exactly is a brand? According to how-to-branding.com, a brand is described as 'the sum of everything your organization is, says, and does'. This includes your logo, your website, your brochures, how you (or your team) answer the phone, the tone and type of language you use, and more.

Essentially, it is the experience people have of your company—for customers, this ranges from their initial enquiry to after-sale support. For suppliers, this includes how you brief them and whether or not you pay on time. For partners, this encompasses the approach you take when working together.

When done well, branding creates the reputation you want in the marketplace and helps to attract the type of customers that are a good fit for your products. When done poorly, it either leads to a negative reputation in the marketplace, or no reputation at all because people can't remember who you are and what you stand for.

Creating a brand is not simply about creating a logo, although that is the central visual representation of what your company stands for. Having followed the steps in Chapter 1 you have a good understanding of what your business stands for (your why), what you want to achieve (your vision) and how you will operate (your values). The missing link, in terms of branding, is investigating how your business will fit into the marketplace. What makes your business different from all the others that operate in your space? How will you communicate this difference?

All these elements—your why, vision, values and point of difference—then need to be encapsulated into your name, logo and tagline and carried across the different material that your company produces, from product descriptions to help information, your website, brochures, signage and any other visual information. Having clarity about each of these elements is a great place to start when it comes to briefing a graphic designer for a new or updated logo.

Your branding also needs to be congruent with how you operate, in particular, what systems you put in place to support the promises you make with your brand. If, for example, your point of difference is 24/7 after-sales support that you offer your customers then you will need to implement systems to ensure you can deliver on that key promise. If you don't do this, in other words, if you say one thing in your promotional material but can't deliver then this results in mistrust and reluctance from potential customers to do business with you.

THE POWER OF CONSISTENCY

Once you have a clear brand identity, the key is to ensure your branding is consistent so that each time a customer or potential customer interacts with you they receive the same message.

One thing I've seen some companies do is having minimal flair on their main website and saving all the 'personality' for social media. There is a disconnect with taking this approach and, as a small business, you've worked hard to get a visitor to your website or social media page and you don't want to confuse or push them away by crossing from friendly to corporate and un-engaging or vice versa.

Instead, consistency is key to creating a strong, memorable brand. Brand consistency will help differentiate your business from your competitors, increase customer recognition and reinforce what solutions you're offering. This then makes it easier for people to remember you; the more consistent you are across different mediums, the stronger that impression will be.

This is even more crucial for small businesses that don't have the luxury of correcting any confusion through large-scale advertising campaigns or a media blitz.

If you already have branding in place, try this test to determine whether your branding is consistent and understood—simply ask your employees what they think your brand and company represents. Do their answers tally up, or do they vary considerably? If they vary, you may have a consistency problem.

So how do you create consistency in your branding? Ensuring that your brand is consistently represented doesn't just happen by chance. The best way to ensure this consistency is by putting the key elements of your brand together in one easy-to-access reference document. Let's call it your brand guide.

Your brand guide doesn't have to be a long and overly prescriptive document, but having things in one place does make it easier for everyone in your business to maintain a consistent approach.

You can include:

- Preferred fonts
- RBG color codes used in your logo
- Where to locate your latest logo on the company shared drive
- Your why, your vision and your values, in other words, what you're trying to achieve for your customers
- Your brand voice—how would you describe it? Is it helpful, casual, clever, relaxed?
- Preferred email signature so it's consistent across all employees
- Business card sample layout
- Graphic designer contact details
- Printer contact details
- Login details for any websites used by marketing

You can download a sample copy of a brand guide from harbren. com to see how this can look.

This document can be given to new employees and a modified version (without login information) to any marketing suppliers to give them an introduction to your branding or placed on an internal shared drive or intranet.

Does it always need to be the same?

Of course, being consistent doesn't mean it has to be exactly the same. For example, you can vary the wording to describe your brand or your logo on different pieces of collateral to suit the occasion.

Google is one example of an easily recognized brand that continually alters the way their logo appears, depending on what is happening around the world. This makes Google seem in touch with and responsive to current events, a handy and desirable attribute for a search engine.

For example, they adjust their logo to include a birthday cake if you are logged into a Gmail account and use Google search on your birthday. Other changes to the look of the word 'Google' correspond with international events like Christmas, Easter or Valentine's Day. After Philip Hughes died and the practice of leaving a cricket bat outside the front door became a common practice, Google had an image of a cricket bat resting against the 'G' of Google.

However, there are a couple of points to note about the changes that Google makes. Even when they change the look of the logo itself, there are many elements that remain the same. The location of the wording on the page above the search box and the search box location remains consistent regardless of the color and imagery.

Brand consistency comes from keeping everything in a similar or complimentary tone. For example, having a crowded brochure or website that has many areas competing for attention would be jarring for a brand that espouses simplicity and a minimalist approach.

Similarly a product that is designed to make life easier needs to have supporting information that is in keeping with that aim and isn't overly long or difficult to interpret. Ikea is an example of a brand that consistently struggles with this. They promote their products as being easy to assemble but their customers don't always agree and they have become fodder for comedy with the many failed results.

YOUR BRAND VOICE

Another aspect to consider is finding a 'voice' or personality that sits well with you and your brand. I recently read a book about motivation by Dr Jason Fox called *The Game Changer*, which discusses how to use game design to 'shift behavior, shape culture and make clever happen'.

Throughout the book are cartoon drawings that help to illustrate the points being made in the text. Some are whimsical, some fun and they complement the unique voice Dr Fox brings to his writing. This style is carried over onto his website and his 'museletters', his word for his infrequent email newsletters.

While having a distinctive voice can make you stand out, you don't want it to be so unique that you're the only one who can carry it off. It needs to be one that can be replicated and communicated to others.

The main benefit of having a clear and consistent brand voice is that it creates a connection and becomes, over time, instantly recognizable to your customers. This is important because people connect with people, they don't relate directly to a company but rather the people behind the brand and company.

Murder Burger is a New Zealand burger bar with a distinctive brand voice that they use on all their communication, even job ads. They recently posted an ad with the headline "Murder Burger Needs More Meat". The advertisement is a very honest account of the responsibilities and benefits of working for the company in line with their promise on the about us page of their website of a 'real' burger without any "artificial flavors, colors, and god knows what else".

Go-To Skincare created by Zoe Foster Blake, a well-known beauty editor and author, has created a brand voice that reflects her quirky and irreverent personality while still maintaining her credibility as someone customers can trust. On her website she describes the company as "skin care minus the confusion. There are no irritants or nasties, no faux-science ("Now with added Wrinkleflickatox™ and Moisturemagic® particles!") and no outrageous claims."

Done well a brand voice becomes a shortcut to connecting each time customers interact with you. This provides a degree of comfort that they are in familiar hands and you can solve their problem because you understand them.

The key to developing a brand voice is knowing your customers so that you can speak to them using a particular tone and language that will resonate with them and being authentic so that the personality portrayed is a true reflection of your offering and isn't just faked to get the sale.

Some questions to ask to get your brand voice right for your company:

- Do we sound the same on the phone as we do in our written communication?
- What annoys our customers?
- What do they respond well to?
- How do customers respond to different personalities within the business?

In reviewing the answers to these questions, you'll get a feel for what the best match will be. Often your brand voice is something that develops over time as you become more confident and get ongoing feedback from customers.

GET YOUR STORY STRAIGHT

Storytelling probably isn't the first thing that comes to mind when considering your marketing approach, but when you think about it stories are how we communicate and connect with others. From the yarns you hear over drinks, the recounting of sporting exploits and the mishaps of camping holidays, to the stories we tell each other and ourselves about our day, stories play a key role in our everyday lives.

Stories make us laugh, they make us feel—nostalgic, sad, happy, excited, frustrated, relieved—help us make sense of the world and help us share our experiences with others.

This is why creating and refining your brand and company story is an important step in breaking out of your turnover rut and getting some attention from your target market. Telling stories:

- Builds trust
- Sells the benefits of your solution
- Establishes credibility, and
- Makes it easier to encourage word of mouth

Most importantly, stories connect with people.

People generally don't feel warm about or attached to a company. Instead, they connect to the people and the stories *behind* the company. Telling stories shares who is behind the scenes making things happen and driving the business forward. This then makes stories shareable.

Let's compare two businesses based on their stories, as an example. ProjectShoe.com and ShoesofPrey.com both offer custom designed shoes for women. They both have a great range of options, ordering is done online and they have easy to navigate, well laid out websites. At first glance there is little that sets them apart.

However, one key difference is that the About page called 'Get to Know Us' on ProjectShoe.com is impersonal focusing on the product and the ordering process not the people behind the brand and why the business was set up.

"Welcome to Project Shoe, the online destination that puts shoe designing in your hands. Founded as the premier source for personal shoe design and customization, Project Shoe provides you with the tools to turn your creative visions into reality. Here at Project Shoe, you can imagine your very own, custom footwear using our elite design tools and an endless selection of high quality materials so that your ultimate dream of designing the perfect shoe can finally be realized."

By contrast, ShoesofPrey.com is more forthcoming. Jodie Fox, co-founded the company with two ex-Google employees, because of her interest in trying to find shoes that were just right:

'I was solving a problem of my own. I'd always liked shoes, but I never loved them because I couldn't find exactly what I was looking for. Either it wasn't quite the right color, there was an embellishment I didn't like, not quite the right heel height. When I was travelling, in the same way that you find someone who will make a custom suit for you, I found someone with whom I could commission shoe designs. My shoe collection became really exciting, and my girlfriends asked me where I was getting my footwear. When I explained, they asked me to create shoes for them too.'

Which company would you be more likely to order from and tell your friends about?

Finally, storytelling doesn't cost an arm and a leg, making it especially useful for small businesses wanting to get cut through in the sea of big-budget branding.

But before we talk about how to put your brand storytelling together and the different elements involved, let's start with how to *find* your story.

FINDING YOUR STORY

In 2005, Steve Jobs gave a commencement speech at Stanford University, where he described his life experiences as a series of dots. It was only looking back over his life that he was able to see how the dots connected to form a cohesive narrative, and how everything he had experienced contributed to who he had become, and what Apple had become.

One example was dropping in on calligraphy classes in college, which had a direct impact on the aesthetics of all his products and on the development of fonts.

Like Steve Jobs, everyone has a story of how they got to where they are and a unique take on life as a result of those experiences. This could encompass what you've done, how you did it, what you learned or why you did it. It's only by reviewing these experiences that you can start to connect the dots and form your own story.

Some general questions you can ask yourself to begin uncovering your story include:

- What experiences have you had that are unusual?
- How do your experiences impact your product development?
- What problem do you solve?
- Why are you the best person to solve this problem?
- What is your unique combination of skills?

To put this into perspective lets go through an example. Helen Wust Lock has created a skincare company, XMA Therapy. Here are her answers to each of the questions:

- What experiences have you had that are unusual?
  My sister Wendy was forced to stop working as a nurse because of her eczema. I wanted to develop my own moisturizer, one with a blend of ingredients that I could pronounce, that were edible and would offer my sister some relief.
- How do your experiences impact your product development?
  I was working in the coffee shop at the Royal Brisbane Hospital and I started offering the eczema cream to staff at the hospital and they reported back that it cleared up their skin unlike anything else they'd tried.

- What problem do you solve?

  Rob, a Pilot started using his son's XMAcream on long haul flights and the flight attendants were all using it too, saying that it was great for keeping skin hydrated. I did a bit more research and adjusted the blend slightly and another product, Aviation Hydration was created.

- Why are you the best person to solve this problem? What is your unique combination of skills?

  I'm naturally inquisitive and I'm very focused on natural remedies where possible. It was really my sister's experience which prompted me to find a skincare solution.

  I was diagnosed with arthritis when I was 25 and was put on the same drugs as my father who was 50. I needed a walking stick because my knee kept giving out on me. My parents sent me off to Queensland because they thought the warm weather would help.

  I wanted to go the natural route because I didn't want to have years and years of drugs. I had to read a lot of health and nutrition books and do my own research to find alternatives. I became known as "Dr Lock" within the family because of all the reading I did.

Let's put that together in a story:

Helen Wust Lock began experimenting with natural skincare solutions when her sister Wendy was forced to stop working as a nurse because of her chronic eczema. Helen, known in her family as 'Dr Lock', because although she doesn't have any formal medical training has long been an avid reader of health and nutrition books. This quest for alternatives began when she was diagnosed with arthritis at 25, handed a walking stick to stop her wayward knee and put on drugs, the same drugs her 50 year-old father was also taking. Not wanting to face a life of medication, she began exploring natural options.

Through her research she was able to devise a diet, nutrition and supplement regime that dramatically relieved her symptoms and meant she was able to ditch the walking stick. She applied the same determination and inventiveness towards her quest to help her sister. The result was a moisturizer with a blend of 14 natural ingredients that were easy to pronounce, edible and offered her sister some relief.

Helen was working in the coffee shop at the Royal Brisbane Hospital at the time and started offering her unique eczema cream to staff at the hospital. They reported back that it cleared up their skin unlike anything else they'd tried. XMA cream and a fledgling business were born.

Rob, a pilot, started using his son's XMA cream on long haul flights. He found it was great for keeping his skin hydrated. He then started buying more XMA cream for the rest of the crew. This led Helen to undertake more research and make some adjustments to the blend before another product, Aviation Hydration, was created.

TIP:

If you're not sure what is memorable or noteworthy about your story, start noticing what other people, particularly those who fit your target market, share when talking about great products they find. Do they start with the product or the owners behind the brand? This should help you to see where to put more of your effort and provide ideas on how you can frame up your story.

STRUCTURING YOUR STORY

In fiction, there is a maxim that there is no story without conflict. While your life may not have had the high drama of a Shakespearean tragedy, thinking about it as a narrative from a structural point of view can help to uncover it.

This involves covering four key areas—your problems, challenges, triumph and evolution.

Business ideas often arise as a result of personal or professional frustration. It is this frustration with the way things currently operate that generates both the idea for a business and the motivation to make it happen.

To find the 'problem' part of your narrative, think about:

- What was your big frustration and why was that important?
- What was the catalyst behind the development of your first product or service?
- What prompted you to start your business?

Next come the challenges you faced on the journey to solving those problems. The story of Edison inventing the light bulb and trying thousands of different prototypes before getting it right is a more memorable and engaging tale because of his attempts that didn't work. If Edison had simply invented a light bulb that could be used on a mass scale without any struggle, the story wouldn't be nearly as compelling as the story of his dogged persistence to get it right.

Another good example is James Dyson's story about how he worked for five years and produced 5,127 prototypes before finally creating the world's first bag-less vacuum cleaner. This is now a part of Dyson folklore and is an integral selling point for their products. The underlying message is that if Dyson has created something new then you know that it will be good as it has undergone rigorous testing to get it right.

This is why it's important not to gloss over the effort involved in finding your solution, particularly those problems that were a threat to you getting started and have now been resolved.

To find your challenges, ask yourself:

- What did you try?
- What worked, what didn't?
- Why didn't it work?
- What problems did you encounter in bringing it to market?
- How long did it take?
- Did you think about giving up? Why didn't you?

The triumph is when you overcame those challenges. This could be the breakthrough moment when you discovered the solution to the problems you discovered earlier, or could be when you successfully brought that solution to the market.

This is a crucial part of your story because this is the payoff, both to you and the person reading or listening to your story. The reader is looking for that reward, the upside to all the challenges and frustrations of launching a new product. They want to feel the excitement of finally getting your product in the hands of a customer.

It's also a way, through quoting or summarizing the customer feedback you received, to reinforce why your product is the solution the reader is looking for, as well as a way to ease them into reading other customer testimonials.

To craft your triumph, think about:

- When did you discover the solution? How did it feel?
- When did you make your first sale? How did you feel?
- What was the feedback from customers like?
- What success have you experienced since then?

The final stage of the story is your evolution. This aspect of your story is about keeping the reader engaged and excited about what you will come out with next. It may trigger them to bookmark your website or request a brochure for later use. Think about:

- How has your product changed?
- What other products are you working on?
- What else is planned?
- How do you ensure you keep innovating? Do you read particular magazines, follow certain companies, attend trade shows or conferences, workshop with your team or something else?

While you may not end up including all of these points, this serves as a useful guide for working out the structure of your story. Editing down a story to a document that flows well is easier to do if each aspect is fully covered upfront.

HOW TO GET YOUR STORY OUT

There are many ways you can pick to get your story out of your head and onto the page. The way you choose will depend on your particular style and whether you're a visual person, a talker or need interaction with someone else.

Using the questions listed in the previous section, try the following methods to get your story out:

- **Recording audio**—using a recording app on your phone or computer, you can record yourself talking and then get it transcribed and edited later. If this is your preferred method then imagine you're sitting down with a good friend with amnesia and you need to summarize what you've done with your life.
- **Mind maps**—this approach can work well if you're a visual thinker as it allows you to dump all the related elements onto the page or screen and then put them in order later. The mind map becomes the scaffolding for your content that you can then go through to flesh out each point.

- **Working with a writer**—this is good if you work better with others and think as you talk. The writer can ask you the questions listed in this book or come up with their own. Once they have your answers, they can then turn them into a usable document.

TIP:

If you do decide to work with a writer or editor, it's important to make sure that your story doesn't become so glossy that it loses its soul. Share your mistakes, the times you thought you'd found success and it eluded you, the near misses and how you responded to those setbacks. People want to get to know you and your brand; they don't want to be stonewalled by corporate speak and clichés.

SHARING YOUR STORY

Once your story is polished and you're happy with it, then share it with your employees and suppliers. Employees need to know it so they can properly represent who you are and what your business stands for to your customers. Sharing it with suppliers can help to build a relationship with them. Both can be good sources of feedback on what may need tweaking to get it customer ready.

CREATE YOUR PRODUCT STORY

The storytelling doesn't have to end with the owner and why the business was created. You can create memorable details around your products as well. This is important as it shows that each product is purposefully created to solve a particular problem that customers are experiencing and isn't a random product produced to increase sales.

Lululemon does this well. On each product page, under the heading 'Why we made this', they provide information about why each product was created, who it was designed for and the intended use. Together with specific information on the fabrics, features and benefits, this helps place each item in the minds of their customers as well as demonstrating that they aren't just mass-producing the latest fashion piece like every other retailer in that space. Instead, they are providing products that fill a particular need.

Because they have given a detailed 'story', if I was talking to a friend who said they were looking for a pair of shorts that didn't chafe during running then I could recommend Lululemon as they have several products that fit that requirement.

The other key benefit is that product stories help build trust and connection. Because Lululemon are talking about how they are overcoming a particular problem that their customers are experiencing, they demonstrate a high level of understanding of their target market. If a customer purchases that product and it does solve the problem then they will be more inclined to believe claims about other products that the company makes.

There are two elements required to create a compelling narrative about your products. The first is the benefits of each product, and the second is what makes them unique in the marketplace.

WHY SHOULD THEY BUY YOUR PRODUCT?
FEATURES VS. BENEFITS

Do you explain features or benefits when you discuss your product with customers? Do you know the difference between the two? If not, don't worry—you're not alone.

A feature is a quality of your product—this may be a physical quality, or some functionality. A benefit, on the other hand, is the reason why this should matter to your customer—how the feature will solve a problem or improve their lives.

Let's take a drinking bottle, for example. A feature of the bottle is its pop-up lid. The benefits of this lid include:

- Customers can hold liquid in the bottle without it going everywhere if it's knocked over or moved.
- It prevents the liquid in the bottle from being contaminated by smells in the fridge.
- It prevents bugs or debris from dropping into the liquid.
- Customers can easily hydrate while they work out (this isn't so easy with screw-top bottles).

Another feature might be that the bottle is dishwasher-safe. The benefits of this include:

- The bottle is easy to clean.
- Using the dishwasher saves your customers time.
- It protects their health, as easy cleaning helps keep harmful bacteria at bay.

A third feature could be that the bottle is made from BPA-free plastic. The benefits?

- Using the bottle is better for their health, as they avoid the dangerous toxins that leech into water when using other bottles.
- The taste stays pure.

See the difference?

If you don't currently explain what the benefits are for each of your product features, it's time to start thinking. List the features of each of your products and, for each feature, list why each one is beneficial for your customers.

Some questions you can ask are:

- What is the end result for the customer?
- How does it help them?
- What problem does this feature solve?

You may not use all of these details in your marketing material, but being clear about what they are is a good first step.

WHAT MAKES YOUR PRODUCT UNIQUE? YOUR USP

Once you have a clear list of benefits, the next step is thinking about what makes your solution unique.

While there are many BPA-free dishwasher-safe water bottles with pop-up lids, the unique selling proposition, or USP, will be the thing that makes your bottle different to everyone else's. In the example above, there is little that makes this bottle different from other similar bottles. A difference could be the look of the bottle, perhaps it comes with different football logos, or has a unique pattern that makes it more appealing.

However, while this may make it stand out, it is not an enduring USP as it would be relatively easy for a competitor to copy and then a customers' decision on which bottle to choose comes down to price. Assuming all other features are the same, which bottle is cheapest?

A more compelling USP for the bottle would be one that set this particular bottle apart. One that had a microbial coating that was safe to drink but ensured the bottle didn't harbor any smells or micro-organisms could be a good USP. Or perhaps one that gave a reading of how much water had been consumed for the day, accounting for refills so that a user could accurately monitor their water intake.

The benefit of having a strong USP is that it clearly answers the question of why a customer should buy your product rather than a competitor's and moves the focus away from price.

It is the rationale behind why your solution exists and should guide you in both shaping your key benefits and determining which particular benefits to highlight.

Your USP should be your most compelling benefit or a summary of your benefits. When it comes to your marketing, this will lead any discussion of your product, whether that discussion is on your website, in a brochure, or is used in a pitch.

SUMMARY

Once you are clear on who you are and what you stand for in your business, the next step is to consider how you express this through your branding, business story and product story.

Having a consistent brand means that any time a potential customer sees you in the market place, they will know exactly who you are and what you stand for. If they are your target market and have a need for your product, they are likely to be drawn in by the look and feel of your offering.

By contrast, if you don't have a consistent brand you will struggle to stand out and be memorable in the fight for customers.

Clear business and product stories make you relatable. They are one of the most (if not the most) effective way of connecting with your customers, and make your business and products memorable and shareable.

KEY ACTIONS

Review your branding

- ❖ What makes your business different to your competition?
- ❖ Is your branding consistent and in keeping with your why, vision, values and point of difference?
- ❖ Do you have systems in place to support your brand promise?
- ❖ Create a brand guide so everything is in one place
- ❖ Do you have a distinctive brand voice? What would work best with your customers?

Create a compelling story

- ❖ Create your company story by explaining the problems, challenges, triumph and evolution of your business
- ❖ Explain why each product was created and how each one solves your customers' problems.
- ❖ Review the features and benefits for each product.
- ❖ What is the USP for your products?

CHAPTER 3

KNOW YOUR CUSTOMERS

I n the first two chapters I covered what was interesting about what you're offering and how to incorporate that information into your marketing material. This chapter is about better understanding who your customers are so you can reach them more effectively with your marketing.

KNOW YOUR CUSTOMERS

You've been in business for a while and you've developed a solution around a particular problem or set of problems. But have you taken a step back to analyze who your customers are? Not the ones that you *thought* would buy your solution, but the ones who *did*?

This is an important distinction because often consumers use a product differently to how it was intended. For example, the internet was initially used by universities to send messages to people in other universities but the first significant adopter of the technology, once it became available to the public, was the porn industry.

So, take a moment to reflect on your current customers.

- Who are your customers?
- How old are they?
- Are they male or female?
- How much do they earn?
- What's their marital status?
- What are their hobbies and interests?
- Where are they located? Rural, urban, local, international?
- Where do they hang out? Online or offline?
- What do they typically do or think?

The factors you pick and how deep you choose to go will depend, to a large extent, on the type of product you're offering and how challenging it is to categorize and reach your customers. The key is finding the traits they share, so you can effectively group them. So, if your customers are an even split of men and women between the ages of eighteen and sixty in both rural and urban areas, then you'll need to consider other attributes that they may have in common. These might include:

- Psychographic factors—lifestyle, personality, motives, attributes
- Behavioral traits—brand loyalty, usage, price sensitivity, product expectations
- Typical interaction with your brand—do your customers typically come to your business, buy what they like and leave or do they usually ask a number of questions before they pull out their wallet to buy?

Knowing this information will make it easier to target your marketing to potential new customers. For example, if your customers make buying decisions quickly and simply, having clear product information and imagery and a straightforward purchase process are areas that you need to focus on. If they prefer to ask questions before making a purchasing decision, you'll need a comprehensive FAQ page on your website, multiple ways to contact your business (social media links, phone number, email address and physical address) and downloadable product information as well as guides on how to get the most out of your product.

If you don't have this information, it's time to start researching! One way to get those details is to survey your existing customers and find out. You can offer an incentive (a prize or reward) to encourage customers to complete it if you think it may be difficult to get enough participants.

NARROW YOUR FOCUS

Once you know your existing customers, the next step is to narrow your focus to target a single group or niche.

The main advantage of focusing on a single group, or niche, is that you can target your marketing directly to that audience and their particular problems. This means that you can tailor your marketing materials so they speak directly to that audience and you can then share those materials in the places where that audience is most likely to see them.

This has two benefits. Firstly, your marketing is cheaper, because you aren't paying to advertise in areas that your target market might not see. Secondly, you get a better conversion rate, as your marketing will speak directly to your niche's pain points. One common marketing maxim is the key to success is to find out what people want and then give it to them. The better you understand whom your customers are, the easier it is to do that.

This then increases the trust your target market has in your ability to solve their problems and allows you to design specific solutions for specific challenges.

By contrast, if you try to appeal to everyone your message can get lost in a sea of blandness. Generic statements sound unclear, unfocused and typically don't address the specific concerns of your customers.

Let's say that you created a new type of saucepan that better distributes heat to the food being cooked, which saves your customers time and uses less energy than using conventional saucepans. At first glance, your market could be anyone who cooks food. However, that is a competitive space with big brands like Le Creuset, Scanpan, Raco, Baccarat and many more all competing for customer dollars.

So, how can you narrow down to gain a foothold in the market?

In this instance, a group that would be interested in this product might be well-educated mothers who have just had their second child. This is often a time when life speeds up exponentially because they already have one child (often a toddler) and need to prepare food for them while also tending to their new baby. They could use the microwave, but they have concerns about how safe it is when preparing food. Also, finances are usually stretched as they are earning the same amount (or more likely less if they've dropped to one income and have limited maternity leave) yet have increased their outgoings. They would likely be interested in a saucepan that offers a fast and safe alternative to the microwave while using less energy and saving money on cooking costs.

By targeting this particular customer, you could then be more specific in the language you use to ensure your marketing has a greater impact. For example, if you ran a focus group for new mothers, these groups would likely involve discussions around how chaotic evenings are now they have a second child. Everyone is tired at this time of day but they want to do the 'right' thing and prepare healthy food for their toddler. The challenge is trying to find a safe, affordable way that doesn't take forever to cook so they can quickly get food on the table for their irritable and impatient toddler and still have time to tend to the needs of their newborn.

By contrast, if you targeted the camping and caravan market as customers instead, that niche would have different priorities. Rather than focusing on health, they would likely be interested in a product that cooks faster and uses less gas. Therefore, their focus groups would likely talk about how they get frustrated at running out of gas and they don't want to spend lots of time preparing food because they would rather be relaxing or enjoying outdoor activities like fishing or hiking or sightseeing.

As you can imagine, the language and imagery you would use would change depending on whether the target was the camping niche or new mothers of two children. While the problems of each may seem the same at a glance—both would benefit from a faster and cheaper cookware solution—how each group would describe their problems is very different. You could have outdoor shots for the camping niche and language around how the saucepan would allow them to get back to the great outdoors with less fuss. For the new mother niche, you could have imagery of a mother reading to her toddler while breastfeeding her baby and discuss how this innovative new cookware gives families cost savings and a way to prepare healthy food quickly so they can get on with the rest of their evening.

In working out the best niche for your business, you can ask the following questions:

- Who do you most like working with or having as customers?
- Which customers are the most profitable for your business?

- Can you easily identify this niche? Do they have some definable characteristics that would make them easy to find?

Once you've identified which customers you'd like to focus on, the next step is to consider their preferences and how they behave. What do your target market like to read, watch, do and listen to?

Reverting back to our earlier example, the new mothers are likely to:

- Read—magazines like Parenting magazine, websites like NewParent.com, CafeMom.com, Babycenter.com.
- Watch—TV shows like Offspring, Grey's Anatomy and children's movies & TV shows (anything by Pixar, PlaySchool).
- Do—go on Facebook to share photos of their children, meet up with other mothers at cafes and parks.
- Listen to—they may struggle to get their own time to listen to anything other than the Wiggles but when they do they crave thinking radio shows like AM.

Of course, the above is a generalization and there will be customers that are in this target market that don't match all of the examples listed. The aim of this exercise is to get a better understanding of your customers, their problems and where they can be found, not to create a 100% accurate dossier.

Once you have built a profile on your ideal clients then its time to start brainstorming their problems and frustrations. List out as many as you can and then group them into three key areas. Some questions you can ask to uncover these problems:

What frustrates them most? What do they complain about? What is important to them? What do they want more of? What do they want to do but can't?

What keeps them awake at night?

Knowing your customers' problems is key to being able to communicate with them. New mothers are often frustrated at having little time to themselves while also wanting to do the best they can for their children. This means spending precious downtime, usually when their children are having a nap, navigating through all the conflicting advice they read. The real problem is knowing who to trust or what to believe.

For you, as a saucepan company, to solve this problem you could focus on building trust in your product and demonstrating that it is safe to use and does do what you say it will. This can be done through customer testimonials, case studies, statistics that support your time and cost saving claims and by associating your brand with sources that this target market already trusts. For example, you could create a press release and submit it to BabyCenter.com that highlights the time and cost savings for new parents that come from using your saucepan. This highly targeted approach is far more likely to get you noticed than a general press release that only focuses on how innovative the saucepans are.

If you feel like there are a number of customers who currently buy your solutions, the best way to start is by focusing on which one of those groups has the most potential for growth. Then, once you've established yourself as the go-to company for that niche, you can expand your reach.

EXPAND YOUR REACH

One of the common fears around niching is that you might miss out on potential customers who don't fit your chosen niche. In fact, the opposite is true—by having a clear niche, you can serve that niche more effectively, which means you're more likely to have a broader appeal than if you had tried to appeal to everyone in the first place.

Narrowing your focus only to expand again may seem counter intuitive, but taking this approach gives you the ability to gain traction with one demographic, which will then support your growth as you target the next one.

Take the example of a personal trainer who specializes in working with vegan body builders. Although he is targeting a fairly narrow market segment, it will be easier for him to become well known because while there are a lot of personal trainers, there isn't a lot who focus on vegan body builders. Then, once he builds a reputation within that niche, non-vegans are also likely to be attracted to his approach. After all, if he can get results with a vegan diet, imagine what he could do with someone on a regular diet!

There are many examples of leading brands using a narrow approach to gain traction before expanding into larger niches as the company grows. Facebook is one. When it started it targeted students at Harvard interested in connecting with their fellow students. It was then expanded to other Ivy League schools, to all colleges in the USA and Canada and, finally, to anyone around the world over thirteen years of age.

Similarly, Jim's Group has evolved from the narrow focus of lawn-mowing services to establishing a broad national network in response to market demand. The business started out as one person, Jim Penman, offering mowing services as a way to supplement his income while he studied for his PhD. It has since expanded through franchising to include thirty-six other services beyond gardening. And while the range of services offered to customers has grown, the target market for franchisees remains focused on people who want to be their own boss within the security and structure of a larger group.

SUMMARY

For a business to effectively attract and serve its customers, it must first know those customers. By knowing your customers you can target your marketing to them, which makes it more likely that they will respond by enquiring, buying your product or connecting with you online.

In a small business, knowing your customers isn't enough— you need to commit to serving a small niche. Big businesses can afford to be generalists as they have the budgets and reach to market to a general market—online, in print, on radio and on television. As small businesses don't have that market or that reach, it makes it difficult to compete. Instead, focus at becoming the best at serving one particular type of customer—then word will start to spread among that customer type.

Even while you are focusing on a particular market niche, it doesn't mean that you can only service customers that fit your criteria.

Once you have built a reputation in your niche, *then* it may be time to consider expanding your reach to focus on other niches.

KEY ACTIONS

❖ Who are your current customers? Think about:
  • Psychographic factors—lifestyle, personality, motives, attributes
  • Behavioral traits—brand loyalty, usage, price sensitivity, product expectations
  • Typical interaction with your brand—do your customers typically come to your business, buy what they like and leave or do they usually ask a number of questions before they pull out their wallet to buy?
❖ What customers do you like working with? What customers are most profitable for your business?
❖ Create a profile of your ideal customers. Think about:
  • What do your customers like to do, read, watch and listen to?
  • What are their problems? List as many as you can and then summarize them into 3 key areas.

CHAPTER 4

TURN YOUR IDENTITY
INTO COLLATERAL

O nce you have a clear brand identity and a clear niche, the next step is re-examining your existing marketing collateral, or creating new collateral, in the context of your identity and niche. This will ensure you present your brand consistently and in a way that is more likely to appeal to your target market.

In this chapter, we'll look at your website, brochures, content, video, audio and interactive marketing collateral to ensure they are all sharing the same messages and are effectively drawing more customers into your business.

WEBSITE

According to Mashable.com one of the top five reasons a visitor will leave a website without clicking on anything is because the site doesn't clearly communicate a business's brand. Therefore, a good website should encompass everything I've covered so far—who you are, your brand identity, your target customers and their desires.

From the perspective of your brand identity, everything on the site should be there because it adds value to the brand, your message and your product. Your visitors should feel like they are getting to know you as they navigate the site, rather than being stuck in a non-descript, corporate template.

From your customers' perspective, the role of your website is to convince them that you can solve their problems. Think about your current website (if you have one). Is it immediately clear that you understand your website visitors' problems and how you can assist? Do you demonstrate how you can help them get what they want? No? Then you've already lost them.

By contrast, if it's immediately clear that your website can solve your customers' problems, this invites them to keep looking. This invites them to scroll down, to click through to different pages, to watch videos and to read descriptions. Ultimately, this should persuade them to take the action you want them to take, whether that's to buy a product, contact you for more information, or to find a retailer.

While this should be addressed in all of your marketing collateral—brochures, videos, articles and more, the value of having a website is giving your visitors the ability to immediately take action.

In order to do this, your website needs to have a clear purpose to be effective. This purpose is usually the action you want your visitors to take, as listed previously. Once you are clear on that action, your website can be designed to make it as easy as possible for your visitors to take that action.

This means your website needs to be functional and intuitive to navigate—a website that looks fabulous but is infuriating to use is not going to engage visitors. What you want to avoid is a site full of special effects because you're after that sci-fi cutting edge kind of impression. You're better to stick to practical and appealing rather than so edgy that your message gets lost in gimmicks.

Depending on how your business is structured your website maybe used more to capture leads that are then followed up by your sales team rather than to directly make sales. If the purpose of your website is to generate leads, then this may mean having a sign up area where visitors can enter their name and email address in return for receiving a regular newsletter or a special report. Or visitors maybe encouraged to complete the online contact form. Other sites work more like an online brochure by having the phone number or email address prominently displayed and encouraging visitors to make contact directly with the company. Many service companies have websites like this.

Transactional sites, that is those that sell products directly to customers, are typically more complicated as they need to have the ability to receive payment and all the follow up tracking and processing to ensure payments are processed and products delivered.

KEY PAGES FOR YOUR WEBSITE

A basic business website should include the following pages:

- Homepage
- About
- FAQs
- Testimonials (this could also be incorporated into the About page)
- Contact
- Product page

Homepage

The home page is usually the most visited page of your site because it's the page that most traffic is directed towards. It can also be the only page visited if it doesn't invite more investigation.

When a visitor arrives at your website, it is like they've entered your showroom. This is your opportunity to demonstrate what you are all about and how you can help them. However, there are a few key differences between a web visitor and an actual visitor to your premises. For one thing you can do without the formalities like saying 'Welcome, how are you? Isn't it hot outside...'

They aren't interested in chitchat because they don't need to be. They are one mouse click away from leaving your site; because it's not a physical location they don't need to think about social niceties or worry that they'll offend you if they walk in take a quick look around and walk straight out again.

They want you to get down to business straight away and engage them in 3 seconds or less. What they most want to know is what's in it for them, why should they stay instead of clicking away?

The purpose of the homepage is to showcase how you can help and entice your visitor to click deeper into your site. The key elements of a home page are a great headline, images of the company and products together with short introductions to the rest of the website. For example, there is usually links to other pages on the site with more detailed descriptions of what you offer, brief summary of your business with a link to an About page, a sign up form for a newsletter or report as well as full navigation menu that links to the other key pages on the site.

TIP:

A headline that sums up how you can assist is one of the best ways to quickly engage with a visitor to your website. For example,

Canva.com is a design-oriented website and the first thing you see when you land on the homepage is two endorsements—'The Easiest to Use Design Site in the World' and 'Canva enables anyone to become a designer'. This immediately tells visitors the purpose of the site, but also reassures them that the site is suitable for non-designers, too.

Proprofs.com makes it easy to build training and testing programs and has the following headline on their homepage, '1,214,000+ businesses, educators and students trust our tools for building & testing knowledge!' Again, this demonstrates the purpose of the site and also provides some proof that other people have found their system effective, making it more compelling for the visitor to find out more.

This can take a bit of brainstorming to get right. It should be succinct and cut to the core of your solution. The main focus of the headline should be around the Unique Selling Proposition that we covered in the last chapter.

About page

For many of my clients, the About page is the most commonly visited page after their homepage, so it shouldn't be underestimated in terms of its importance.

People want to know who they are dealing with, both from a security point of view (particularly if your site is a transactional site) but also out of curiosity about who is behind the brand.

Your About page provides context for web visitors and anchors them to your solution. It is also your opportunity to let your customer get to know you, which makes it the perfect place to integrate the story you created in Chapter 2.

TIP:

To get started writing your About page, use the answers to your story in the previous chapter or answer the following questions:

- Who are you and what do you offer?
- How do you deliver this solution?
- Why was the business founded and when?
- What is your point of difference?
- What action would you like your visitors to take once they finish reading?
- What are your customers' main challenges?
- What are some customer success stories?
- What credentials do you have that makes you an expert at solving your customers' problems?

FAQs

This page needs to list out all of the frequently asked questions that your customers ask. Usually if one customer asks a question then they'll be others that have the same question but, for whatever reason, don't ask. Think of these questions as objections that your customers are posing before they commit.

This page is your opportunity to deal with those objections that your visitors may have so that you can both allay their fears or concerns and confirm your understanding of their problems. Doing this in an effective manner means that you'll then be able to either keep them on your site longer or they'll feel comfortable reaching out to start a conversation about how you can help them.

TIPS:

- If you don't currently have a FAQ page ask each of your staff members for the top 5 things that customers ask them. Use this as the starting material for the page and update the page as new questions arise.

- If you have a lot of questions and answers consider grouping them under headings and list the headings at the top so users can quickly navigate to the information they want.

Testimonials

A testimonial page is the place to share experiences that other customers have had when using your product. This feedback or social proof is important both in terms of credibility and understanding. Customers derive a degree of comfort in knowing that your solution has worked successfully for others and they can also get ideas and tips on how best to use your product.

Testimonials don't just have to be written. Video testimonials are becoming more common and can work better at conveying the passion your customers have for your product.

TIPS:

- To be considered authentic and credible testimonials need to be direct quotes from your customers and, where possible, include some basic identifying information like names and suburbs or companies.

- The more specific customers can be about their experience in a testimonial the more useful the feedback is for other potential customers. Feedback from a customer saying service was great is not as compelling as a comment about how patient the salesperson was and how quickly they were able to help them work out what product would suit them best.

Contact

This page needs to present a number of ways for customers to contact your business: email or online contact form (or preferably both), phone, postal address and social media links. If you include a physical address then include a map.

Also including the name of the person who will be responding to any enquiries is a personal touch that creates a degree of familiarity and distinguishes your business from a large corporate or automated service.

TIP:

If you have an online contact form, test it regularly to ensure that it works. Also make sure that there is confirmation on screen when a message has been submitted and an email confirming receipt and contact details for the customer to follow up if they want or need to.

Product page

This is the page where you need to go into greater description about your product, in particular, what it does, how it works, who uses it and how they use it. This page is your opportunity to explain why your product is so great and how it can help your customers to solve their problem.

If you're printing a brochure or catalogue then the expense involved will often limit the number of images that you display. However, when it comes to a website, apart from the upfront photography costs there is little excuse for stopping at one photo per product, particularly given that most photographers usually take multiple photos of each product to get the best representation.

Another idea is including product videos, which works well for fashion products where customers want to see what a product looks like when it's being worn.

One company that has great images and videos on their website for each product is Bellroy. Bellroy make wallets that use less leather so that the wallet is slimmer and takes up less bulk in a pocket or bag

On most websites for wallets, you'll find photos of their wallets closed and opened. On Bellroy's website they have videos that demonstrate how each product works and what can fit inside it. This is important for backing up their claim of being slimmer yet still offering ample room to store all the usual items carried in a wallet. They also have multiple product images including a photo of the wallet with its packaging (an important consideration if the product is brought as a gift).

TIP:

Include as much descriptive information about the product as possible, particularly information about what the product is made from, the exact dimensions, care instructions or how often the product needs to be replaced.

DIY OR PROFESSIONALLY DESIGNED?

While getting a website custom made for your business may seem like the best solution, there are several drawbacks to this approach:

- It can be considerably more expensive to get a custom design rather than adapting an existing template or system to suit. Chances are that what you want to do has been done before, so this may not be the best investment.
- If you decide to change web developers then all the know-how about how the system works is lost unless you get detailed

documentation along with the site (rarely viable as most sites usually undergo constant iterations and updates).

- Updates to the system to cope with browser upgrades can't always be implemented site-wide with one easy click and will often need to be done by the developer at your expense.

- Communicating exactly what you want when building a site from scratch is a complicated and time-consuming process and, if you decide to pursue this option, you'll need to be very clear about what you want and devote time and energy into fine-tuning the site until you get it.

In most cases, I recommend doing it yourself (or having someone from your team do it) using a basic WordPress template, known as a 'theme'.

I like WordPress because it offers you the flexibility to install extras to enhance the usability of your website (a bit like getting extra apps for your smartphone), it is easy to change the look of your website with a pre-designed theme, most of the new WordPress themes are optimized for mobile browsers, there is a lot of free support available online if you run into problems, most web developers are familiar with it (in case you choose to use a developer), the backend interface is easy to use and it has the flexibility to set different access levels for different users.

Regardless of the system you choose, the key things to keep in mind are whether or not you and your staff can make quick, simple changes, or whether you'll be reliant on a third-party web designer to do it for you, and whether the platform can grow with you as your business grows.

TIPS:

- Be clear about the purpose of your website—is it about encouraging visitors to contact you for more information, to buy direct or find a retailer? Whichever option it is make it easy for users to get what they want.

- Even though your About page is about your business, everything on it needs to relate back to your customers.
- Do you have an unusual spelling for your business? If so, consider buying other domains with misspellings for your name and then re-direct visitors to your main website. That way, if a user has heard from a friend about your site but misspells the address, they will still be able to locate you.
- Consider buying other variations of your domain, like .com if you only have the .org version and vice versa if you only have .org. Common spelling mistakes can also be good ideas for domain names. For a few extra dollars each year, this will ensure that potential customers who enter the wrong one will still find your site.

BROCHURE

Traditionally businesses put out brochures to explain who they were and what they could offer. With the move to online, many companies now opt to put that content into a website because it's much easier to update, saves on printing costs and can be made available to a wider audience.

However, there is still a place for a printed brochure (as well as having a PDF version online). As well as being easier to share or show others, having a summary of what you do that is tactile can provide additional credibility for your business.

It's important to be clear about the purpose of your brochure and how it fits into your sales process. While the point of a brochure is to sell what you do, you may find that you need a few different options to fit in with a potential customer's progress through your sales funnel. For example, you could have one that provides a general overview with the aim being to entice the reader to find out more information or motivate them to have a sales conversation, and another brochure that is used during a sales conversation that is more detailed and works as an order form with space for credit card details.

In terms of size and layout, there are many options that you can choose from. You could create an A4 booklet, single A4 flyer or it could be a smaller folded or concertinaed flyer. Different formats are needed depending on how you're planning on using it, the preferences of your target market and the amount of information that you want to display.

For example, if you're creating a flyer as part of a letterbox drop campaign in a particular geographic area then it's important to structure your information around a special offer. This is because you're competing with many other direct mail pieces and want to have an offer that will first grab the attention of the recipient and secondly, make them get in contact to continue the conversation or complete a transaction.

In this example, the size of the flyer will depend on how many options you want to promote. Pizza companies like Dominos and Pizza Hut usually go with a multiple page A5 flyer as they display a number of food and drink package deals. This type of brochure is heavily focused on price and value. The length of the flyer is determined by how many deals they want to show. Too many offers will confuse customers, too few and there may not be enough options to cater for different customer preferences.

If you're planning on sending out a brochure along with a sales letter to potential clients in a direct mail campaign then a longer multi-page brochure with good quality photos may work well. This type of layout provides an opportunity to go into greater depth about your product offering and how it solves your customers' problems. However, a multi-page brochure can add to the cost in terms of design, printing and postage.

Many brochures focus too much on the company and not enough on the benefits for the customer. Like your website, a brochure needs to primarily be about your customers, about how you understand the problems they are experiencing and how your product or expertise will help them.

A multi-page high gloss brochure I saw recently had headlines like 'Our Clients', 'Our Expertise' and 'Our Work'. These headlines and the content were all about the company, there was nothing about what that expertise meant for the reader, nothing about what to expect if this company was hired and no information to illustrate that they understood the reader's concerns. What they could achieve for new customers was inferred (if they've achieved great results for others then they could do it again for a new customer and because they have all these resources and skills they can handle any customer problems). They'd gone to a lot of time and expense to put the brochure together but left the key takeaways up to the reader's ability to deduce what they meant.

The key elements of different types of flyers are:

- Offer based brochure
  - headline that explains your offer & key benefit
  - product image
  - short description of what is involved in offer
  - call to action/next steps
  - contact information
- Company Booklet
  - headline that sums up what your company offers & unique selling proposition
  - images (product images, logo)
  - who you service
  - 3 key customer problems
  - how your solution works and how it solves your customers problems
  - the benefits of using it

- o testimonials and case studies (if appropriate)
- o background information on company
- o contact information
- o next steps

Whether your brochure provides an overview or focuses on one particular product or range of products, you need to consider:

- Your target market—what style will work best for your customers? High gloss with a premium finish and lots of photos or something more utilitarian with a focus on the facts?
- How will it be distributed? Will it be mailed out or handed out at a trade show or from your showroom? Or will it be part of a letterbox drop campaign? What design and layout would make it stand out from other direct mail pieces your potential customers currently receive?
- What do your competitors' brochures look like? Is yours noticeably different? Or do customers often confuse your company brochure with your competitors?
- Need to have a clean and easy to read layout with headlines to breakup the text and entice the reader through the content.
- Booklets should be done in multiples of 4 after you go past one double-sided page, for example, 1,2,4,8,12,16 etc to account for paper size and print layouts.

TIPS:
- Use great images as well as content.
- Get professional help to create the content and design. It is worth getting an experienced copywriter and designer to put your brochure together.

- Have your content written first and be clear on the purpose of the brochure, target market and how you're going to use it before getting a designer to work on design and layout.
- Be as focused as possible with the content—it doesn't need to include every bit of available information. The aim of a brochure is to start a conversation or initiate a transaction, not educate the reader on everything that you do.
- Including testimonials and case studies where appropriate provides credibility and is seen as proof that you can be trusted to deliver on your brand promise.
- Ensure that you have clear instructions on what to do next to start a conversation, find out more or make a purchase.

CONTENT MARKETING

Content marketing has become more popular in recent years, but many don't really understand what it means. Content marketing simply refers to the creation and distribution of information designed to attract and engage potential customers. It can take many different forms, but some common examples are articles, blog posts, podcasts and videos.

While content marketing is a technique to promote your business, it is primarily about creating material that you can distribute via different platforms. Where advertising focuses more on selling and action, content marketing is a more subtle informative approach and can be very effective.

There are a number of advantages to this marketing strategy. It gives you the opportunity to build rapport with potential customers— there is a considerable difference between the amount of time that a potential customer spends with your brand if they are reading an article or listening to a podcast compared to how long it takes to scan an advertisement. The other key difference is that in the latter they know they are being sold to. By contrast, the former feels more like they are being informed and they are therefore less likely to have their defenses raised.

Content marketing helps establish your business as expert in your field, which then leads to more business at higher prices. With more of your content available online there are more opportunities for people to find you. Finally, good content has longevity—an article can continue generating traffic months (even years) after it is published.

The disadvantages are that while it may not cost you to place content on other websites, in newsletters or on your own blog, there is still a time cost involved in creating and generating the content itself as well as the effort spent promoting the material so it gains awareness and popularity. It can feel like a slower approach than directly advertising, as the benefits of this strategy usually build up as more content is created and distributed. Finally, without solid processes in place to continually feed the content furnace, it can be difficult to sustain a content marketing strategy.

What sort of content should you create? Some ideas include articles, blog posts, PDFs, audio files and videos about the following:

- Common mistakes that people make when buying or using your products
- The usual mistakes that cause buyers' remorse in your area
- Discussion of the three key problems that your customers typically experience
- Reviews of related products
- Checklists
- Discussions on trends or innovations in your industry
- Interviews with industry leaders or trendsetters
- DIY tools like templates, frameworks, and how-to guides
- Mini-courses on how to get the most out of your product

- Survey results that would interest your market
- Quizzes and self-assessments for business or personal use
- Case studies of clients who love your product

Simply ask yourself what information your customers need to get the most out of your product. How can you help them use your product more and gain the benefits?

CUSTOMER-DRIVEN CONTENT

Some products also lend themselves to customer-driven content. For example, GoPro is a product that is designed for customers to create their own content. In turn, this content becomes a promotional tool for the company.

The key with this content isn't simply promoting what your customers are creating, but ensuring that this content accurately reflects your brand identity. As a result, you will need to have people who can curate, moderate and monitor both the content and the feedback it generates.

If your product doesn't naturally lend itself to customer-generated content, it may still be possible to encourage customer engagement through activities like competitions and the use of hashtags on social media. For example, if you have a business that creates products for the home like Snowden, then you could create a hashtag like #SnowdenTeaCups and ask users to share their favourite teacup to use with their Snowden Teapot. Customers can then take photos of their cup of choice alongside their Snowden Teapot and share them on Instagram, Pinterest or Facebook. This type of tactic increases your product's exposure while letting people show off their own styling choices. Another idea is focusing on customers' favourite spots to enjoy a cup of tea from their Snowden Teapot.

TIPS:

- Create a plan for generating content so that you can get some consistency in terms of output, themes and placement.
- Pay attention to what works best to stimulate customer engagement and use those insights to direct the creation of new content.

VIDEO

Both customers and businesses are increasingly using videos as broadband speeds improve, and this medium is expected to become even more important over the coming years.

Why? Videos are a great way to build rapport, increase trust and get your message across. MrYScribe, a company that creates animated whiteboard videos, claims that the average length of time that a visitor remains on a website increases significantly when a video is added to the site: 'A whiteboard animation video will increase your audience engagement by more than sixty-five per cent.' Many also find videos more engaging and memorable than just reading content.

However, the cost of producing professional videos is significantly more expensive than having a few articles written, and a lot of planning around what will be said and shown is required before filming to ensure you get a good result. This is particularly applicable if the video is a piece about product or company features and benefits. If the video is more casual, then less planning and scripting is required, but there will still be time spent editing it into a cohesive piece.

TIPS:

- Keep it short (less than two minutes) particularly if it's a company overview video or focuses on a particular product. If you're creating interviews or how-to guides, then they can be as long as they need to be to achieve their purpose.

- Open with a shot of your logo and close with a call to action.
- As with other collateral, be clear about the purpose of the video and, unless you have chosen an edgy, hand-held vibe, get an experienced video production company to help create the videos you need.

When picking a company to use, look at material they've created for other companies and note what you like and dislike so you can give them clear guidelines about what you want.

Useful tool:

- Camtasia is a recording and editing package for videos. It's relatively easy to use and offers a thirty-day free trial so you can try it out. Another one that is good for screenshots is Screencast.

PODCASTS

Podcasts are like online radio shows and feature people talking about things that interest them, and they are distributed through third-party services like iTunes and Spotify. Some podcasts are re-purposed from elsewhere, like radio shows that are edited down to remove all the music so you only hear the host(s) talking, while others feature original content like interviews.

Podcasts can be a great way to build rapport with your audience. Podcasting also gives you an opportunity to position your business as a thought leader in your space and gives you continual exposure to your target market.

However, there is time involved in creating content and lining up people to interview as well as recording the show itself and then editing and producing the finished product. If you decide to upload your podcast to a distribution service, it's also important to make an ongoing commitment to the show.

So if you've decided to try podcasting, what do you talk about? Podcasts can cover a range of topics, with the categories on iTunes including comedy, radio drama, true stories, technology, games & hobbies, business, science, news & politics, music, literature, film, design, kids & family, and fascinating facts. The key is to choose an area where you have something to say and can credibly position yourself as a thought leader, and to ensure you have a fertile stream of content to draw on. This might include interviews with your customers if they are doing interesting things with your product, or you could interview related companies in your area (a personal trainer could schedule chats with other health-oriented services like naturopaths, dieticians, physiotherapists and chiropractors as well as call on other fitness trainers specialising in particular techniques like kick-boxing).

TIPS:
- Have several episodes of content lined up before you launch.
- Be clear about the audience you are targeting and choose content to suit them—what category will appeal most to your target market?
- Work hard to promote your show in the first few weeks so that you will be featured in the 'trending' area of iTunes—you have a brief window of time to appear in this area and need to make the most of it if you want to build a new audience for your business.

If the idea of creating audio content appeals to you but you're not sure about doing this on an ongoing basis, you can still create a podcast and use it as way to offer an alternative option for your customers to connect with you, rather than using it to directly build an audience. An alternative is to record and stream audio on your website. While you'll lose out on the possible promotion opportunities that you could get through a distribution service, you'll still be making interesting content available for your web visitors. This will keep them on your site for longer, draw them back to see if you have created anything new, or prompt them to sign up for your email mailing list to find out about any new content you publish.

Useful tool:

- Audacity is an audio editing tool that can help to streamline your audio, remove background noise and cut the 'ahs', 'ums' and pauses so that your podcast sounds more streamlined.

INTERACTIVE RESOURCES

Interactive tools include things like games, quizzes, self-assessment tools and even apps. These tools are a great way to increase engagement with your customers, to enhance the use of your product and to create an experience that your customers want to share and talk about.

For example, if you create wearable technology like a Garmin sports watch, then having your own app that has a reporting function makes sense as it can enhance the usability of your product as well as creating a greater degree of 'stickiness'. If a customer has two years' worth of running data available through their Garmin smartphone that they can quickly access and track improvements, then changing to a different brand of watch is a bigger decision than just getting a new timepiece to wear. A change means they 'lose' all that data and start over with new stats. They also have to get used to a different way of operating the watch and the reporting app. So a new watch would need to offer considerably more benefits than their current one for a user to make a change.

Magnum Pleasure Hunt was an interactive online game created to increase customer engagement. It worked. According to Inc.com the game attracted around 20 million plays because it was fun to play and managed to keep the product as a key part of the gaming action.

HowToFascinate.com uses an online quiz called the Fascination Advantage Assessment as a way of engaging visitors to spend more time on the website and provides an opportunity to follow up with them. The 5 minute test is completed by the user answering a series of questions without any identifying information. However, to receive the results, contact information including email address is required. The benefit of doing a test like this is that not only does it seem natural to ask for contact information so that the user can receive the test results but the company also now has a detailed profile on the type of person they are. The company can use that information to tailor how they communicate with that user in the future. For example, if the results indicate that the user values innovation then they can ensure that the follow up emails emphasise how the results of the report can be used to inspire innovation in others.

However, although these tools and gadgets have a lot of value, they can take considerable time and money to create and, if not well thought out, they can detract from your core product.

TIPS:

- The best place to start is to take an existing process or step in your sales process and turn it into an app or online quiz. Even if you don't get any new customers by developing these tools, they will have the potential of reducing costs by streamlining your processes. You'll also gain valuable experience about what works and what doesn't and can use that knowledge to branch out for your next interactive tool.
- Be clear about the purpose of the tool before you create it and consider how you will promote it and encourage your existing and potential customers to use it.

- Get feedback from existing customers before finalising the tool and again, after you've launched. It will likely take time to get it right so that its as useful or engaging as possible.

PUTTING IT ALL TOGETHER

The goal of creating this collateral should be increasing your business's sales and turnover. The mistake many small businesses make is just creating a website, starting a podcast or printing some brochures and then hoping that alone will lead to more sales.

The key is using your collateral to create a sales funnel.

A sales funnel is the journey a customer takes when building a relationship with, and ultimately buying from, your business. This funnel has a number of levels, starting with free and inexpensive information and products, and progressively offering more valuable products and services as the relationship develops.

An example of a traditional sales funnel might be that of a bricks-and-mortar jewellery store. This might involve having different price points of products in their store so that a customer can buy cheaper items before working their way up to more expensive pieces. A more modern take might be offering a free guide to purchasing jewellery, which is available for download on the jeweller's website. This could then be followed by a series of emails that share the stories and expertise of different artisans who create the bespoke jewellery in store, followed by an invitation to participate in a sale on some lower-priced items.

As you can see, each step in the funnel allows potential customers to steadily become more familiar with you, making them more likely to purchase one of the higher-priced items later in their journey.

This process is referred to as a funnel because it tends to narrow as potential customers flow down to the next level. At each level, the funnel weeds out the tyre kickers so that only serious contenders remain.

By measuring your results at each level of the funnel, you can increase your conversion rate, thereby increasing your sales.

While this does involve some time and expense to set up, once created, the effort to maintain these assets is very low as the entire process can be automated. The payoff is usually a higher conversion rate. The other benefit is that you're creating shareable content that can help to spread the word about your business.

TIPS:

- Just because you may be offering the information products in your sales funnel for free, don't skimp on design or content. Have information that is useful, offers value to the customer and looks professional and appealing.

- When working out what to offer, pick the information that will most appeal to your target market. In the above example, it wouldn't make sense to offer a buyer's guide to opals if you sell relatively few of them and they don't appeal to your target demographic.

- You will need to have a third-party email setup to handle the delivery of free, digital content automatically. Some popular email distributors include Aweber, MailChimp, Active Campaign and InfusionSoft.

- If you have a retail outlet, consider creating a print version of your free guide that customers can pick up in store. You could then offer to sign customers up for the next stage, the email series. This is a way to gather their contact information and keep them moving through your funnel.

- Make sure you have information about your company in any of these information products—background information, website, contact details are the basics you'll need.

SUMMARY

There is a wide range of marketing collateral that you can create to engage with existing and potential customers. Some, like a website or brochure, are basics that are expected or sought after.

Others like visual material, audio and interactive tools are optional but can greatly enhance your market's awareness and understanding of what you offer.

KEY ACTIONS

- ❖ Website actions
  - Review your website to see if you have the basic pages covered—Home page, About, FAQ, Testimonials, Contact, Product pages.
  - Is it clear what the next steps are for your web visitors?
- ❖ Brochure actions
  - Review any existing brochures—do they cover the key points? Do they focus on helping your customers or is it all about you?
  - If you don't have one, what sort of brochure would work best?
- ❖ Content
  - Review what content you currently create— does it work to engage your customers?
  - Go through the list of possible content creation options and consider what content to create that would help to educate potential customers.
- ❖ Video actions
  - If you have videos available, do they work to engage customers? How can they be improved?
- ❖ Podcast actions

- Would this appeal to your customers? Decide if it's worth pursuing as a way to engage customers or build an audience.
- If unsure, create some brief question and answer audio, upload it to your site or to social media and see what the response is like.

❖ Interactive resource actions

- What process could you automate through an app or online tool?

CHAPTER 5

PICK 'N' MIX YOUR MARKETING PLATFORMS

Y ou've now thought about the material that you could create to better convey your brand. The next step is to work out how you'll use that material to connect with your target market.

However, there are many different marketing techniques that you can use to promote your products and business, so it's not surprising that many business owners are confused about which options they should pick. Is letterbox marketing better than email marketing? Do bus billboards perform better than banner ads on a media website? Twitter or Facebook? It seems that every day there is a new method you 'must' adopt to have any chance of success.

Picking the right platform for your message is just as important as what you say. The wrong channel with the right message is a dilution of your efforts and a waste of resources. By contrast, sending the right message through the right channel will lead to your message being seen and shared, which will lead to more customers coming to your business.

In this chapter I'll cover off a few of the key areas you have to choose from like referrers, email marketing and social media, as well as things to think about when choosing the right platforms for you.

REFERRERS

Finding referrers to promote your products can be a great strategy for small businesses with limited resources they can devote to marketing.

They may take many different forms, both paid and unpaid. Referrers could be third-party affiliates, formal partnership arrangements, your staff and distributors, directories and even search engines.

Third-Party Affiliates

In any affiliate arrangement, you pay for each lead or sale generated by a registered affiliate. In less-formal partnerships, this could be paying someone a commission when they refer a customer to you, while third-party networks like Clickbank.com and ShareaSale.com share the deal you're offering with their network of members or affiliates, who can then choose to promote it. If an affiliate generates a lead or sale (you decide how the payment will work), they will then get paid a flat rate or a percentage for each lead or sale they create.

The advantages of this sort of system are that you can quickly mobilise an army of sales people to work for you on a performance basis with minimal setup. You can also set guidelines for how your product will be promoted and what methods your affiliates can use.

However, there are disadvantages. When using a third-party network, you run the risk of some affiliates promoting your brand in ways that damage the long-term credibility of what you offer if they use misleading copy. You are reliant on the network to properly screen affiliates and you are reliant on the tracking capability of the network to accurately report lead and sale activity. This then leads to the extra work of monitoring and updating your own tracking so you can corroborate their figures.

Ultimately, this approach works best when you know what the lifetime value of a customer is to your business and, therefore, how much you can pay for each lead or sale and still make a profit. If you are paying per lead, this approach works best when you have a well-developed sales funnel and can reliably convert leads into sales.

TIPS:

- Review which other companies are currently using the third-party network you're considering using. If possible, reach out directly and ask them about their experiences and whether they would recommend the network.
- Ensure your sales tracking is setup properly before you start so you can verify the data the network is providing.

Partners

Marketing partners are those who send you leads and customers. You may have an affiliate (this could be paid or unpaid) or a reciprocal arrangement where you also send them leads and customers. You can also offer joint promotions by packaging your products, whereby you both win with every sale.

The main advantage of partners is that they are a great way to cost effectively reach your target market. This is particularly applicable if you don't have a large database of customers and want to leverage both the credibility and customer base of another company.

When choosing a partner, the ideal situation is to find providers of complementary products that have the same target market as you. That way both of you have access to and can provide value to similar customers without competing.

If you're promoting saucepans to the caravan market your potential partners could be tent and caravan manufacturers, portable stove companies or caravan equipment suppliers.

Working out how to structure this arrangement to get the most benefit for both businesses can take a little tweaking. Running a few tests at the beginning can help with this process. If you take this approach, make it clear that they are tests to see if the arrangement works for both sides. You don't want to be locked into an agreement that becomes more work with limited benefits.

A media partnership that I negotiated for a client started out with the media company wanting access to my client's email database in exchange for online advertising and sending a message to their database of 8,000 subscribers. This was of interest but we were unwilling to message our list until we had seen how responsive theirs was. The mailout resulted in less than 200 clicks and no sales which was surprising given the size of the list and how targeted it was. However, the partnership did open up a productive dialogue and we were able to get several articles published in their online magazine.

TIPS:

- The key to making partnerships work is understanding what benefits you both expect to get out of the arrangement and what value each party brings to the relationship. The ideal situation is a win/win/win—a win for you, a win for your partner and a win for your (joint) customers.
- Take the time to get to know potential partners before launching in to discussion of a working arrangement. This can avert costly mistakes and give you a better understanding of how much time and effort to commit to the relationship.

- The clearer you are on your target market, the easier it will be to find partners that either attract or target the same target market.

Sales Staff and Distributors

If you have your own sales staff then they need to be familiar with your branding, your story, your collateral and your sales message so they can be consistent. It's important to avoid a mismatch between what your collateral says about your business and what your sales staff are saying.

If you don't sell direct to customers then your distributors are a key marketing channel. Again, they need to understand your collateral, sales message, story and branding. And, as they are an extension of your brand, you need to choose them wisely.

It is also not wise to leave all the selling up to them without any input or advice. It's in your best interests to help them sell your product so make it as easy as possible with things like staff training, in-store demonstrations, marketing collateral, appealing point of sale stands, feedback on techniques that work well and information on the target market that you feel is most suitable for your product. The better educated your distributors are about your offering, the better they will be able to sell it to others.

TIPS:

- Randomly sit in on sales calls or meetings that your staff are making to see if they are in alignment with your brand message.
- If your products are sold to customers by a retailer, visit the store and observe how the sales staff talk about your products. Is there any obvious misunderstandings that you can fix with training, better merchandising or collateral?

Directories

There are a number of directories online that can be used to make your business more findable. These range from general ones like True Local and Yellow Pages to more specific ones like TripAdvisor and UrbanSpoon.

Many of these directories are free to list in and it is worth adding your business details to these sites to help get your business in front of more potential clients. To ensure they work for you, make sure that you keep a listing of what you've added so that if anything changes, for example, you move offices, these listings can be quickly and easily updated.

TIP:

Monitoring the traffic received from directories is important when deciding whether to gain more prominence and upgrade to a paid option.

Search Engines

Search engine marketing comprises two areas—your organic search ranking (where your page appears in a search engine's results when someone looks for a keyword or phrase related to your business or offering), and paid search advertising (these are the results that appear at the very top of the page and in the right-hand column). For now I'll focus on your search engine ranking, and will discuss paid search advertising under *Online advertising.*

Being ranked well in the search engines is called Search Engine Optimisation or SEO. It is about being found when someone types in a key term related to your business. For example, if you enter 'Brisbane Accountant' into a search engine then you'll see a list of companies that have a focus on 'Brisbane' and 'Accountant' on their website.

The advantage of focussing on ranking on the first page of the search engine results for a particular term or phrase is that it can bring in a regular stream of highly relevant traffic to your website, people that are actively searching for what you're offering.

The disadvantage of SEO is that it is an inexact science. There are a number of factors that contribute to ranking and they are the subject of vigorous debate among SEO professionals. The debate arises because it can seem as though the search engines, particularly Google are continually moving the goal posts on what they are looking for. In reality, what they want is the most relevant listings that provide a good user experience for their customers.

Traffic from highly placed listings in the search engines is generally referred to as free traffic. This is because no money has been paid directly to the search engine for ranking your site highly for a particular word or phrase. However, there is typically a cost involved in maintaining a high ranking in the search engines, either the cost of your team's time or an external marketing agency—particularly if the keywords you want to rank for are highly competitive.

TIPS:

- There are steps that you can take as a business owner to improve the clarity of your website and make it easier for the search engines to understand what your site is about but, depending on the nature of your product, this may not be worth devoting considerable resources towards. This is true if your product doesn't fit neatly into an existing category as people are unlikely to be searching for something by name that they haven't heard of.
- Some of the things that Google considers in assessing whether a site provides a good user experience includes quick loading of your site, mobile friendly, contains useful information that relates directly to what users are searching for and is regularly updated with fresh content.

EMAIL MARKETING

Email marketing is where you have a database of existing and potential customers and you send them content by email (this is typically done using a third-party service like MailChimp or InfusionSoft). Visitors either elect to sign up to your email list or you add your customers to your email list by importing an Excel spreadsheet or CSV file. The amount of data that your list contains is up to you, but the minimum is usually a name and email address.

The advantages of email marketing are that you can quickly and easily communicate with your list whenever you want or need to. By using a third-party provider, unsubscribes or profile updates can be handled automatically without any additional admin resources. Once the list is setup and sign up forms added to your site, the entire process is automated, so there is no additional work for you to do to add users to your list. Creating and editing emails is easy with drag and drop design functionality, so all that you need are regular word processing skills to create and edit content. You can also track the responsiveness of your list, including how many people opened your email, who clicked on the links, how many people unsubscribed and so on, which gives you the ability to improve your content.

Many services also offer an autoresponder option, where a series of automated emails can be triggered following an event like a subscription or a sale.

The disadvantages are that it takes resources and time to put content together to send, and if you don't have an understanding of the type of information your customers or prospects are interested in receiving, then it can be a process of trial and error to see what is well received. When using a third-party provider, you also run the risk of losing your data if the third-party system crashes (though this is unlikely with the bigger players). If you receive too many spam complaints it could also result in your account being frozen or shut down.

How Often Should You Email?

The number of times that you email customers depends on your product turnover. It makes sense for fashion brands that have a continual flow of new products to email daily or weekly—they can send an email full of images of their new products, which the customer can quickly click to see more or delete.

For other businesses that don't have such a steady flow of new items, a fortnightly or monthly schedule makes more sense. There is a view that if people aren't unsubscribing to your list then you're not going hard enough. Maybe this is true for companies that are happy to churn their lists frequently, but for most businesses it's about finding that balance between annoying and informative. This will be different for each customer, but a general rule is that if you notice a sharp increase in the number of unsubscribes or a drop in the number of people opening your emails, that is a clue that you are emailing too frequently.

TIPS:

- Give prospects a reason to sign up—Offer something free to entice them to give you their email address, and be clear about the type of content they can expect going forward.

- Deliver on your promises—If you promise a free eBook, course or video series, you need to deliver this in your initial emails. Offering your database different content, particularly in the beginning, would be seen as a betrayal of trust.

- Focus on your subject line—This needs to be compelling enough to get people to open the email.

- Link to your website—Provide plenty of opportunities for people to click within the newsletter. This provides a great way to see what appeals to your database. If you only give them one link to click, then that is not a real measure of how appealing that content is.

- Be on brand—Ensure the layout and branding of your messages is congruent with the rest of your branding. Email providers have templates that you can adapt to suit or you can cheaply purchase alternate layouts.

- Give value before selling—You can also set up a series of automated emails when a user joins your list to educate them on your service or offer tips on how to solve their problem, which helps build a relationship before you try to make a sale.

- Sort your subscribers using filters—From a fee perspective, it's often best to group your subscribers in a single list and then use filters to target your content rather than having multiple lists. For example, filters could be used to send a message to only those customers that live in New South Wales rather than dividing your customers up into separate lists for each state.

- Beware strange code and gobbledegook— Sometimes when cutting and pasting content, the original formatting of your content can create extra code in your newsletter and mess up your formatting. If that happens, cut and paste the information into a plain text editor like Notepad and then paste it back into the system. This doesn't always work but can be a quick fix.

SOCIAL MEDIA

There are a lot of different social media platforms available but there are only six that have scale and need to be seriously considered for small business marketing—Twitter, Facebook, YouTube, LinkedIn, Instagram and Pinterest.

The first reason for focusing on the bigger platforms is that they have a bigger market reach.

The second reason is that you have the ability to be more targeted in your marketing approach by drilling into specific demographics or interests while still having a large enough volume of users to reach out to. Platforms like Facebook offer an amazing amount of specificity when it comes to demographics. For a product like the Bloom Necklace Fitness Tracker from Misfit Wearables, you could set up ads or sponsored posts targeted towards users who meet the following criteria: single women aged eighteen to forty-five who are interested in fitness, have been to university and live in urban areas.

Finally, because it takes considerable effort and resources to stay relevant and connected on these platforms, I don't recommend you dilute your efforts by dabbling in other less popular platforms.

Obviously the top six platforms may change over time as new platforms develop and gather momentum, but as a small business you don't need to be a trailblazer in discovering new mediums until you've gained a degree of mastery over the most popular ones.

Let's look at each of these platforms in more detail so you can figure out which is right for you.

FACEBOOK

WHAT IS IT
Communication and sharing website

OLD-SCHOOL EQUIVALENT
Social section of newspaper

LARGE REACH
936 million daily users (March 2015)

DEMOGRAPHICS
41% are over 35 years (March 2015)

BEST FOR
Directly reaching consumers

Advantages:

- Because of its size you can drill into particular demographics and interests to reach a large chunk of your target market.
- Content can spread quickly, particularly once you've built up a fan base.
- You have the opportunity to catch problems before they develop as you're providing a way for customers to air their problems. This also means you can demonstrate a proactive and responsive approach to solving any issues.

Disadvantages:

- Because content can spread quickly, any errors can be difficult to correct before they catch on, and then a considerable effort is required to recover.
- Facebook is not likely to appeal to business customers as most don't want to be seen to be on Facebook during business hours and the content tends to be more social than professional.
- It can be challenging to continually find new content to put on your company page that is relevant and interesting to your target market.
- Users expect a prompt response to any questions or problems raised, which means your company page needs to be monitored outside normal business hours as well as during.

TIPS:

- It takes work to get 'likes' on your Facebook page so be prepared to devote resources to promote it and offer incentives for users to follow you.
- If you decide to run advertisements on Facebook then test running traffic to your page on Facebook and direct to your website to see which converts better.

PINTEREST

? WHAT IS IT
Photo-sharing website

▣ OLD-SCHOOL EQUIVALENT
Special interest, glossy magazines

◉ REACH
72.8 million users (April 2015)

◕ DEMOGRAPHICS
26% have an income over $100k, 68% of users are female (February 2012)

👍 BEST FOR
Directly reaching female consumers

Advantages:

- This is a great platform to use if you are a service business and have a lot of great photos. Because what you're offering doesn't go out of stock like actual products, any clicks you receive are more likely to result in an enquiry or lead.
- Pinterest works well with visual products.
- You can gain credibility by being 'Pinned' by potential and existing companies.

Disadvantages:

- Users can get disappointed when they click on an image they like only to find that it is no longer in stock. You need to have a way to handle these clicks so that the visitor stays on your site and looks around rather than being so disappointed that they instantly click the 'back' button.

- There is no advertising on Pinterest. You need to become familiar with the language and etiquette used on the site to become successful.
- You can't add a lot of content or description for each image.
- You need to rely on users who pin your content to link the pins back to your site.

TIP:

Users can get frustrated if they click on an image and expect to see the same product available for sale but it's no longer available and all they get is a blank or error page. If you see traffic from Pinterest then consider setting up a unique page to offer alternatives to the product they're seeking.

INSTAGRAM

WHAT IS IT
Photo- and video-sharing website

OLD-SCHOOL EQUIVALENT
Special interest, glossy magazines

REACH
300 million active users (January 2015)

DEMOGRAPHICS
76% of users are under 35 years old (June 2014)

BEST FOR
Directly reaching consumers

Advantages:
- Instagram works well for visual products aimed at women under twenty-five years old.

- An active account with useful and interesting content is likely to result in increased engagement for brands more than with other sites like Facebook and Twitter.
- There is less competition on Instagram compared to Facebook and Twitter.

Disadvantages:

- You can't add clickable links to every update you post so you need to rely on users to copy and paste a URL into a browser to reach your site from a post.
- If your product or service isn't visual then you'll have to work harder or have a solid content plan in place in order to come up with new content and to continue to build engagement and gather new followers.
- All images need to be a square shape, which is not the same as that used by mobile phone cameras, and videos can only be up to fifteen seconds in length.

TIPS:

- Follow other Instagram accounts that you feel will appeal to your target demographic to see what engages them—what gets the most comments and shares?
- Ensure your photos are good quality and interesting to your audience to encourage more customer engagement.

YOUTUBE

WHAT IS IT
Video-sharing website

OLD-SCHOOL EQUIVALENT
free to air and pay TV

REACH
1 billion visitors each month and over 4 billion videos viewed daily (April 2014)

DEMOGRAPHICS
78% of users are males and they spend 44% more time on the site (April 2015)

BEST FOR
Reaching consumers and business professionals

Advantages:

- Videos don't have to be professionally produced to gain traction.
- It can be a good way to upload videos to embed within your own site—this means that you won't use up your own bandwidth every time a video is viewed from your website.
- It can be a good way to increase engagement and build trust with your products and people.
- YouTube is the second-largest search engine and third most-visited website and is increasingly used to find how-to videos. If used well, this means you can position your business as the best solution to your market's problems.
- Having well written articles backed up by complementary videos on YouTube can improve your chances of being well ranked by Google in the search results.
- Sixty-five per cent of people are visual learners, making videos perfect for training materials.

Disadvantages:

- YouTube is very competitive.
- You need to have a clear call to action as there are many other videos to entice a user to click, rather than following through and finding out more information about your business.
- There are advertisements on most videos that can distract users from watching your video.
- A user can't click directly on the video and be taken to your website.

TIP:

Pay attention to the text below your video and provide supporting information like URLs and contact information to make it easier for users to find the information referred to in your videos or follow up with you for more details.

TWITTER

WHAT IS IT
Online message and information service

OLD-SCHOOL EQUIVALENT
Breaking news on TV or front section of paper

REACH
302 million active monthly users (March 2015)

DEMOGRAPHICS
37% of users are aged between 18-29 years (January 2015)

BEST FOR
Directly reaching consumers

Advantages:

- You can follow key influencers for your target market and get their attention directly.
- You can start a 'conversation' with anyone—can be a great way to reach out and build rapport.
- Viral opportunities extend beyond Twitter with news outlets now reporting what people are saying on Twitter as a way of getting direct commentary on topical issues.

Disadvantages:

- To stop problems spinning out of control you need to quickly and empathetically respond to customers.
- Some campaigns can spin out of control quickly and have unintended consequences, thrusting your company into the spotlight in an unfortunate way.
- Twitter feeds can move so quickly that you need to post multiple times each day to gain attention.

TIPS:

- Share other content that you find useful, don't just make it about your products and content.
- Use shortened links like bit.ly so that you don't use up too much of your character limit on your URL. It will also enable you to track how often the links are clicked on.

LINKEDIN

WHAT IS IT
Business-oriented social networking service

OLD-SCHOOL EQUIVALENT
Business and career section of paper, networking functions

REACH
364 million registered users (June 2015)

DEMOGRAPHICS
61% of users are aged between 30-64 years (January 2015)

BEST FOR
Directly reaching personnel within a business

Advantages:

- LinkedIn offers an unprecedented way to get around the traditional business gatekeepers to connect directly to relevant personnel within a business.
- Great for researching a company to see who key personnel are and what activities they and the company have been undertaking.

Disadvantages:

- It still takes effort to build rapport. You can't just connect with people and leave it at that—you need to work it as you would at any networking event and offer value to the other person before they will drop their guard.
- The best way to build rapport is to connect with individuals on a personal basis. As there is no bulk marketing option on LinkedIn, this means sorting all your connections so that you can message each in turn.

- All in all, it can be a more laborious way to build up rapport compared to other social media platforms as the most effective approach is one-on-one personalized messaging.

TIPS:
- Don't rush into sell as soon as you connect with a potential prospect. Take your time getting to know them first.
- Fill out your own LinkedIn profile properly rather than just providing the bare minimum. Potential customers, partners and the media use LinkedIn to research profiles before connecting so it makes sense to be forthcoming about your experience and background.

Regardless of the platform you choose, I advise against using social media unless you make a commitment to resource it appropriately. This is because participation on any of the platforms takes ongoing effort to gain traction and, in my opinion, having a Facebook page or Twitter account that hasn't had any updates for many months is worse than not having it in the first place. Think of it as a living, breathing organism that you must continually feed or it will wither and die. And if it's the latter then, to continue the analogy, the 'corpse' will be paraded publicly for all those interested to see and wonder about.

ONLINE ADVERTISING

Online advertising offers great scope for small businesses and allows them to better compete against bigger businesses with bigger budgets. A second advantage of online advertising is that it is measurable, meaning you can gather a lot of useful data that you can then apply across other mediums like your website and offline advertising.

Because online advertising is both measureable and lower budget than traditional advertising, online campaigns are a great way to test different headlines and sales copy to figure out which products appeal the most to your target market. You can then use this information to improve your conversion rate.

However, it can involve a lot of testing to get it right and you will need to actively monitor campaigns to get the most out of online advertising. It's only through this monitoring that you will be able to act quickly to change copy, images or landing pages to maximize results.

TIP:

Sending traffic to your homepage from an advertisement is generally a waste of time and is less likely to result in a conversion. This is because it doesn't provide a specific solution to the problem the customer is trying to solve and instead requires them to work to find what they want. It is better to set up a specific page (referred to as a landing page) that follows through on the promise set up in the advertisement.

There are three main types of ads that can be run online— banner ads, search ads and email ads.

Banners

Banners appear as images across the top of a webpage (called a leader board), in the sidebar of a webpage or sometimes embedded in the content. Banners are usually charged by the number of impressions or views they receive, with rates quoted by 1,000 impressions.

Although banners are charged on a per view basis, there is no way to measure whether web visitors have actually 'seen' your ad or whether they quickly scrolled down the page without even noticing the banner at the top.

It's also important to keep in mind that the number of people who click these ads are often around just 0.2 per cent of impressions. This means that for every 1,000 times your ad is loaded, you can expect two people to click on the ad.

If the rate you're being charged is six dollars per 1,000 impressions, then it is effectively costing you three dollars for each click, which doesn't seem too bad.

However, that is only the cost of getting visitors to your site. Depending on the conversion rate for your website and your average sale amount, this may not be viable. For example, if we assume you are paying three dollars a click, it will cost you $300 to get 100 visitors to your website. If your website's average conversion rate is one per cent, or one sale for every 100 visitors, this means it is costing you $300 for a single sale.

So if you have one item for sale at $150 then you will be losing $150 per sale on your advertising costs. If the average customer purchases two items with each order, then you would break even. You will therefore only make a profit if they buy more than two items.

TIPS:

- Keep an eye on ad placement and test which works best for your product—Ads that appear above the fold (meaning they are visible on the screen without users having to scroll down) tend to get more views than ads that appear below the fold (ones where users need to scroll down to see it). However, users that scroll down are usually more engaged in the content and aren't leaving the site without really looking at what's on the page. You may find that having your ad below the fold gets less views but the visitors convert better.

- Focus on your target market—If the visitor demographics of a website match your target market, then this is more likely to lead to a return on your investment than a website that targets a different market.

- Choose your artwork carefully—The graphic you use needs to be eye catching with a strong 'call to action' to make users stop, look and click.

- Consider a non-traditional format—Your banner ad doesn't have to be a traditional ad with an image with some text. Instead, consider a text ad with words printed on a white background. Sometimes this can work well as the user is expecting to see an ad, making this non-traditional advertisement more eye catching. Also, use of white space on a crowded website offers some visual relief and can get you more attention and clicks. As always, testing will reveal whether this approach works for your products.

Search

Search advertising involves bidding on particular search terms or keywords, usually via Google, so that when someone searches for that term, your three-line ad will appear at the top of the search results or in the right-hand column.

These ads are referred to as pay per click because you pay only when a user clicks on your ad, rather than them simply 'viewing' or being exposed to your ad as with a banner. This can make it more cost effective. However, competition is more intense for highly sought after keywords, which may raise the price to several dollars per click.

Where your ad appears in the search results, for example, in the first position at the top of page one or on a subsequent page, is a result of the amount you're bidding for each search term and the effectiveness of your ad. As a result, you could have a situation where you pay less than the top bidder but you appear first in the results because your ad is getting more clicks, earning Google more revenue. Your reward for that performance is a lower price and higher positioning.

TIPS:

- Ensure that you have a clear call to action in your ad. Large companies can fund awareness building ad campaigns but small businesses should focus on getting users to take action.

- When a user searches for a particular item in the search engines there is usually other ads as well as organic listings for the searcher to pick. They are looking for the headline and text that most closely matches what they are searching for. To be effective, your ad needs to reflect back the search term in the heading of your ad.

- Think about the words you are bidding on and whether they have alternate meanings. For example, bidding on generic keywords like 'date' or 'dieting' are expensive, highly competitive and in the case of 'date' can have users searching for a variety of topics. A user who enters 'date' maybe looking for a relationship, a calendar, birth records or the release schedule for a movie or book. There is no indication of the user's intent in the phrase 'date' whereas 'date of birth' indicates that the user is looking for information related to a birth record.

- It's important to run at least 2 different ads to see what works best for each phrase. When starting out each ad should emphasize different points. One could focus on price and the other on functionality, timing, prestige or service. The more ads you run then the more choices you can offer potential visitors but the more data is required before a clear 'winner' can be decided on. Once you have a winning message then the emphasis is on improving that message to gain further clicks and customers.

Email

Beyond emailing your own database, you can also advertise to other businesses' and publications' databases.

Once a publication's or business's email list reaches over a few thousand subscribers they will often offer advertising space for sale on a cost per impression basis. This rate varies based on the following:

- How targeted the subscribers are on the list (a list of 10,000 accountants is worth more to a book-keeping software provider than a list of 20,000 financial services professionals)
- How many other ads appear in the email (are you one of five others or are you the sole advertiser?)
- The content of the email (is it crowded with things to click on or is it a considered piece written around one central topic?)
- The frequency of mailings (does the publication email its list daily, weekly, monthly or quarterly?)
- Typical response rates (what percentage of users click on content?)
- Average open rates (what percentage of subscribers normally open their emails?)

TIPS:
- Run a test before committing to an ongoing schedule and ask to run different ads so you can see what works best with their audience. Sometimes this is only possible if you book multiple spots across different messages.
- Subscribe to services to see how the content is displayed before deciding to purchase advertising space. Review the other ads and see if there are any other advertisers that consistently take space, in particular, note any other businesses that are similar size to yours. If they regularly

advertise in a particular newsletter over a few weeks or months then this is a clue that it is working well for them and is worth considering. Look at what they are doing well and what could be improved and apply these points to your own ads and landing page.

OFFLINE ADVERTISING OPTIONS

Although advertising online is a popular choice for many businesses, there are still traditional options available offline.

However, offline advertising does tend to be more expensive. One of the big advantages of digital marketing activities is that typically the upfront cost is lower—you can get started yourself and tweak as you go. By contrast, when marketing offline you need print-quality collateral, which often requires paying a graphic designer to create your ads and a professional photographer to create suitable images.

It's also easier to measure and monitor online activities than offline activities. Users can be tracked online in terms of demographics, location, the way they respond to your advertising, the way they move through the site and a range of other metrics. Offline, however, you have less visibility of how many people have actually seen your ad compared to a pay per click campaign online. This makes testing a more costly operation as you can't continually tweak results by quickly split testing different options.

Finally, another key advantage of online marketing over offline marketing is that the marketing collateral you create can more easily be shared and distributed online for a lower cost. Digital PDF brochures can be sent out to clients via email and promoted through social media links and online advertising, with near-instant delivery, meaning you are delivering the information your targets want, when they want it.

However, offline advertising does have some benefits, the main one being that if all your competitors are advertising online, going offline can be a way to gain more attention. It may also be more appropriate for certain target markets, particularly if your target market is older or in a specific geographic area.

If you think offline advertising is a match for you, your options are newspapers, magazines, flyers and brochures, and display advertising like signage and billboards.

Newspapers

Advertising in newspapers can include a large ad in the main body of the newspaper, a smaller ad in the classified section at the rear, a lift out section or a loose insert. Rates are charged based on the newspaper's expected audience, though cheaper rates per issue can be obtained by making a commitment for a certain number of issues or length of time.

Tracking your success from an ad in a newspaper can either be done by asking new customers where they saw your ad or by creating a different discount code for each ad that you run and then tallying up the responses by counting the number of times each discount code is used.

The advantage of advertising in a newspaper used to be the size of the circulation. With newspapers declining in readership as more readers switch to online this is no longer the case.

However, advertising in a local newspaper can still be a good option for small businesses that want to target a local or regional audience. For example, a consulting client provides auditing services for self managed super funds and his main target market is small accounting firms. In order to reach new markets he ran advertising in the business section of several regional newspapers. The thinking behind this strategy was that accounting professionals in regional areas would be likely to read the local newspaper because they want to stay up-to-date with what is happening in their area and see if any existing or potential clients are mentioned.

TIPS:

- Take a targeted approach and consider ads in either particular sections of a city daily newspaper or a regional newspaper. Unless you have a large budget don't try to compete with bigger businesses by advertising in the front section of a daily paper.
- Include a call to action as you would for an online ad and make sure that you include a URL where they can learn more.
- To track an ad, create a special offer with a unique coupon code so that you can still see where your sales are originating from.
- Ask for sample copies of the publication before committing so you can see what advertisers they currently have and then design something different.

Magazines

Like newspapers, when advertising in magazines you can advertise in the main content pages or in a section devoted to advertiser's products. If advertising in a magazine, you may be able to combine your ad with an editorial (an article that promotes your business written in the style of a regular content piece).

One consideration with running printed full-color ads is the quality of the images you use. Where you can get away with lower-quality photos online, in print the quality needs to be much higher. As a result, the ad will usually need to be created by a graphic designer according to the specs provided by the publisher.

Advertising rates can be high, depending on how broad the market is for the magazine and how popular the title is. Advertising in magazines like Vogue or Harpers Bazaar is out of reach for most small businesses with products aimed at women. However, taking a more specialized approach can yield better results, again depending on your target market. More specialized titles like Public Accountant Magazine can be worth testing if your target market is accountants and you notice a number of competing firms are advertising with them.

TIPS:

- Get back issues of the magazines you're considering advertising in and review existing advertisers. Look to see who is advertising consistently over several issues. Do those companies have the same target market as your business? If so, consider running an ad for a couple of issues to test whether the returns warrant the expenditure.

- Review the other ads and consider how you can make your ad stand out from the other ads on the page. This is particularly important if you're placing an ad in a directory style page towards the back of the publication.

- As with newspaper ads, include a call to action, your URL and a unique offer so you can more easily track leads.

Flyers/Brochures

Flyers and brochures can be distributed by hand through letterbox drops, at events, with your point of sale material or included with any deliveries or purchases.

The key to making flyers or brochures work for you is to make it clear what your product can do for customers and how it can help them solve the problems they are experiencing. They also need to clearly have information on what the next step is for the reader to find out more. Including your website, email address and phone number allows users to quickly access the material they need in the way that best suits them.

The advantage of using a flyer or brochure compared to an advertisement in a publication is that you have a lot more room to explain what your business can offer and you determine the layout and size rather than fitting your message into a pre-determined space. You can also choose the paper size, quality and how it will be distributed.

The disadvantage is that with so many variables it can be daunting working out what will work best. As I've mentioned before a great starting point is to look at what other businesses are doing, particularly if they are consistently advertising in that manner, and see how you can improve on it with your flyer or brochure. For example, if all the brochures or flyers you receive at a conference are A4 size, on white paper and very densely packed with information, then consider creating an A5 flyer that is on colored paper and has one compelling offer surrounded by a lot of clear space.

The other aspect to consider is distribution. For letterbox drops you can either contact a company that distributes direct mail or hire people yourself to do this for you. Going with a company with experience in this area can be a good starting point to find out more about costs and timing so you can then make a decision on what setup will work best for your business.

To include your brochure or flyer in a promotional bag at a conference usually involves becoming a sponsor or taking an exhibitor booth, which involves additional expense on top of the cost of producing the written material.

TIPS:

- If you decide to participate in a conference as a sponsor see if you can combine your flyer/brochure in the promotional bag with a short speaking spot as conference attendees are more likely to consider your promotional material if they've heard you speak.
- Letterbox drops are great for businesses that are targeting a particular demographic area like a restaurant or local legal practice.

Display

Display advertising, like signage, billboard and branded vehicles, seems to be an area that is often overlooked by small businesses. However, depending on your product, it can have a positive impact on your brand awareness and recognition.

When it is done by small businesses, display usually isn't done well. I have seen many small businesses create signage that is difficult to read from a distance, that doesn't provide any contact information and often has no clear call to action.

One sign by a local dentist was on the corner of their practice facing a busy road and had the headline, 'When was your last check up?'. However, it didn't include a phone number or website, which made it difficult for potential customers waiting in traffic to take action. They would have had to make a note of the name of the dentist from the second sign located on a side fence and then remember to follow up when they had time to look up the phone number. By contrast, if the phone number was on the large sign with the call to action on it then the same people could have called from the car while they waited for traffic to clear.

TIP:

While users can't directly click on your ad when it appears offline, including a call to action is just as important as it is with an online ad. A call to action is where you tell the user or viewer what to do. Some examples, are 'phone now for a free consultation', 'click here to read more' or 'visit our website to see our new range'. All of these phrases tell the user how to behave now that they've become aware of your brand, making it clear what the next step is. The text you use for your call to action will vary depending on the focus of the ad and should be changed up to determine what works and so that customers don't zone out and become 'blind' to what you're saying.

CONTENT MARKETING

Content created to demonstrate your expertise, raise awareness of what solutions you can provide and inform and educate your target marketing can be shared or published via all of the marketing platforms covered in this chapter, including:

- Your email newsletter and third-party newsletters,
- Your blogs and third-party blogs,
- Online and offline magazines and newspapers/ sites,
- Social media.

The best approach to get maximum exposure from each piece of content that you produce involves doing a mix of several options listed above. For example, let's say that you run a company that home delivers organic food. You decide to write an article on the latest update by the World Health Organization on the amount of sugar we should be consuming each day because this is a topic that is likely to appeal to those that are health conscious and it also ties in with the new range of low sugar protein balls that you've recently begun stocking.

Once the article is written you could place the article on your blog, send out an email newsletter with a short introduction and a link to the full article on your site as well as posting links to it on social media. You could also create a variation on this article and submit it to health-oriented online magazines. When it appears in those magazines you can then promote it again on your social media pages with a link to it in your next email newsletter. You can also add the logo of the online magazine to your website in an 'as seen in' section on your about page.

TIPS:

- The better quality content you create, the easier it will be to get maximum exposure from each piece of content.

- Create variations of your articles for different publications by adapting each one to suit the audience. This could mean a change to the title as well as different examples in each version. For example, a publication that focuses on young families will be interested in what you have to say about the effects of sugar on children, whereas one targeting retirees will be more interested in the long term impacts of a high sugar diet. These adjustments will earn you respect from the editors of those publications who are continually looking for original content and means you're more likely to get published and asked for additional articles.

DELIVERING ON YOUR PROMISES

Regardless of how you spread the word about your business, it's important to ensure that any promise that is made by a partner, in an ad or in an article is realized once someone reaches your site, calls you or visits your store or office. If not, the customer will be disappointed and they will question whether you are offering the right solution for them.

TIPS:

- Each ad that you place should link customers through to a custom page (also known as a landing page) to continue the conversation that was started in the ad.

- Ensure partners and sales staff are well versed in any new promotions you are marketing.

SUMMARY

Once you have developed your marketing collateral, there are a number of ways that you can attract the attention of your target market and get them to take action. These include referrers, email marketing, content marketing, social media, online advertising and offline advertising.

The first key is knowing where your target market is looking, and choosing the platform that they are most likely to see. For example, if your target market is dentists then doing a letterbox drop to householders may get you noticed by some dentists that happen to reside in the area but isn't the best use of your resources.

The second key is, once you start generating buzz and getting attention from your market, you need to deliver on your promises. Discounts, bonuses and gift vouchers must be honored, your product must live up to expectations, and your referrers must accurately reflect your brand.

KEY ACTIONS

❖ Referrers
  • Do you currently get website or foot traffic from any referrers? Can this relationship be developed to increase the flow of visitors?
  • Do you have any existing partners that refer business to you? What works well in this arrangement and what doesn't? Can you approach other similar businesses about becoming partners?
❖ Email marketing
  • Do you have a database of customers? Consider creating an account with a third party email provider so you can contact your customers to let them know about changes within your business and provide product information.

- If you already have an email marketing setup, review how well it is working for your business and consider how you can improve your results.

❖ Social media
  - Which platforms do you currently use? Are they the right fit for your target market?
  - Review how you interact with social media users and what improvements can be made to increase engagement.

❖ Online advertising
  - Consider trialing online advertising to see what works well to generate leads and sales.
  - Use the information, particularly what ads work better, to shape the information on your other collateral and website. Do some headlines work better than others? Do particular color combinations work better than others?

❖ Offline advertising
  - Take all that you've learnt from your online advertising and apply it to any ads that you run offline.
  - Review what publications are likely to appeal to your target market and see what other ads are regularly appearing.

❖ Content marketing
  - Create a flow chart for how you want to promote each piece of content that is created to ensure you get the most exposure on all the platforms you frequently utilize.

CHAPTER 6

CHOOSE THE RIGHT PLATFORM FOR YOUR BUSINESS

S o now that you know the range of marketing platforms available, which ones are right for your business?

The answer is, of course, it depends. As we covered in the last chapter, the methods you select to promote your business need to be based around what is the right mix for you, not what is trendy or the 'way of the future'. It is far more important to be flexible in your approach and not be rigidly pro one option or the other, at least until tests have conclusively confirmed the best strategy. Even then it's important to adapt as new options become available and new ways of using old options arise.

In recent discussions with a sales trainer about an approach to get cut through for a newly re-branded services business, he discussed the importance of direct mail, particularly when so many companies have switched solely to electronic communication. His recommendation was to send an introductory letter with a 'lumpy' item that related to their service. For example, a branded apron could be sent to potential clients of a food business.

There were a few reasons for this. The first was that the amount of physical mail people receive has reduced dramatically and there is novelty value in communicating in this manner. The second was that sending something that felt different when the user received it and clearly wasn't a bill was likely to make them curious enough to open immediately. And the third reason, and possibly most importantly, was that because the lumpy item would either be one that they kept on their desk or used, it would be an ongoing trigger for their company. It wouldn't just be a one hit use and then forgotten about, unlike an email that can be deleted in seconds.

This recommendation worked for this particular business because they had the contact details for all their existing and potential customers (around 1,000 in total) and mobilizing this type of activity wasn't a huge logistical feat.

So what will influence your decision? Some factors include the type of customers you are targeting (whether other businesses or consumers), how involved you as the business owner want to be in marketing, the resources you have available and the speed with which you want to implement your marketing strategy.

YOUR TARGET MARKET

Your target market is the first thing to consider when choosing how to market. After all, if the purpose of marketing is to connect with potential customers, you want to make sure you're where they're most likely to find you!

For example, if you primarily sell direct to other businesses rather than direct to customers then this will impact which marketing techniques and platforms you use. When marketing to businesses, email marketing can work well but it depends on the size of your customer base and your target market. If you primarily sell to only a handful of distributors then setting up an email marketing system isn't going to be as important as if you have several hundred companies as customers and you'll benefit from the ability to semi-automate emailing them all.

However, the concept behind email marketing, to instantly share company and product information, expertise and special offers, will still apply regardless of the size of your customer base.

When it comes to choosing where to market, the big question is where do your target customers like to hang out? This involves both knowing who your target market is, as discussed in Chapter 3 and knowing their online and offline habits.

Take a moment to think about:

- Which social media sites does your market use?
- Which websites does your market visit?
- Which magazines or newspapers do they read?
- Which events do they attend?
- What are their hobbies and interests?
- How do they spend their weekends?

There are a number of ways to research where your target market might hang out, particularly when it comes to what they are doing online.

Two free tools are Quantcast and Google AdPlanner, which allows you to enter demographic information, interests, market size and get a list of relevant sites, which can spark ideas for sites to approach about advertising.

Another idea is simply going to the big six social media platforms I discussed last chapter and learning about their users. According to BusinessInsider.com.au women are bigger users of social media like Facebook and Instagram than men, but the age demographic for each varies. IBTimes. com states that older users are more likely to use Facebook and under twenty-fives are more likely to use Instagram. This information is freely available and although the stats may sometimes vary between different sites, you're not after exact figures but more a guide on what sites appeal most to different demographics.

Some other ideas to find your target market online include:

- See what ads are appearing on sites or publications related to your business. Make a record in an Excel spreadsheet—if the same ads keep appearing over a period of time then you can assume that it's profitable for the business.

- Survey your customers or web visitors—Ask which other websites they love, ask what they are interested in learning more about, and ask how they would prefer to get updates on your business.

- What attracts attention? Raw numbers are one indication of how appealing a website is but levels of engagement can be more telling. Review content on different sites to see what is drawing the most comments from readers. Do the same with social media posts on topics related to your customers. Look at the number of comments, shares and what type of content attracts the most attention. This will tell you the type of content that readers on that site are most interested in and how engaged they are.

- Check your web stats—How are people finding your website? Who is referring traffic and can you advertise with them?

You can then use this information to choose the marketing platforms that are most likely to have a strong return.

YOUR PRODUCT

If your product is only suited to users in a particular geographic area then it's worth considering both online and offline marketing.

Online, you could reach customers in local areas through geographic targeting on platforms like Google and Facebook. Offline, you could undertake letterbox drops and direct mail along with ads and editorials in local newspapers.

For example, a local suburban restaurant wants to primarily reach potential customers in their local suburb and immediate surrounding areas. While the restaurant may get patrons from further afield if their restaurant or the head chef becomes well known, the bulk of their repeat customers are likely to be locals and should be the main focus for any marketing activities.

Because their main target market is located in a limited geographic area, they can cost effectively employ a number of online and offline marketing activities. Doing a letterbox drop for 5 suburbs is more manageable than trying to cover a whole city that way. They can select only those suburbs that they want to reach when advertising on Facebook and Google. They could also encourage people to sign up for their email list by promoting special offers or competitions both through their website, when taking bookings over the phone and through a physical sign up form on the front desk.

Other activities like writing articles for online food magazines may help to raise the profile of the restaurant but it involves a bigger time commitment and may not result in more local custom. This would be something to explore once other local marketing activities had been tested.

This would also be appropriate if the focus was to build a broader profile beyond the local area to achieve the longer-term growth plans for the business. For example, if the restaurant planned to expand into other geographic and product areas. This could be setting up a new restaurant in another location with the aim of eventually franchising the concept or delivering online cooking classes or selling products (online and in the restaurant) like cookbooks and specialty ingredients.

If you are targeting a select group of people in geographically diverse areas, marketing your offering online is an easier and cheaper way to reach them. If we return to the earlier example of XMA Therapy, it's more cost effective for them to focus primarily on online activities in order to reach eczema sufferers wherever they're located. They could consider running advertisements or writing articles for publication on online sites that target health concerns, as well as those sites specifically focused on skin problems. Facebook could also be an effective platform for promoting and sharing the great results that customers are achieving through the use of the product. Other activities like email marketing would be advisable both in terms of marketing their existing product and to get feedback and suggestions for the development of new products.

YOUR INVOLVEMENT

The next thing you need to consider is how involved you want to be in your marketing. Some business owners like to get involved in the decision making process but want to have marketing activities implemented by staff or contractors, others are comfortable being active on social media and driving ideas for content, and others would prefer to only be consulted on the big marketing decisions so they can focus on refining the existing product range or creating new products.

I've worked with a range of business owners across the involvement spectrum and each approach is fine as long as it's clear what the business owner's level of involvement will be. This is so that the business is resourced appropriately and decisions made about which platforms to choose and the approach to take. For example, if you want to be heavily involved on an ongoing basis then you can be positioned as a 'personality' or thought leader driving the brand. You may choose to contribute ideas, generate content for the company blog, write social media updates, create videos or run a weekly podcast.

If you're a business owner that wants to be involved in the decision making process but doesn't want to be involved in the day-to-day activities then you're going to have to delegate both the marketing activities and the co-ordination of what's happening. This will likely involve hiring staff that can undertake some or all marketing activities and co-ordinate the outsourcing of other tasks as required. You will be reliant on your marketing team to understand your customers. Communicating with customers through podcasting and video blogs are not likely to be activities that your business undertakes as you need a certain amount of authority to carry them off.

Those business owners that want a lower level of involvement would be better suited to focus on low maintenance activities or those that can easily be delivered by others (their own staff and/or contractors as required). These include email marketing where bulk emails can be customized to seem more personal, content marketing through articles written by others, online advertising and referrals from third-party affiliates.

YOUR RESOURCES

The next key influencer on the best activities to promote your product is the resources that you're able to devote to marketing. As with many aspects of business (and life) there is often a trade-off between money and time. The less you can dedicate to your marketing strategy in the form of staff and funding, the more of your time it is going to take to implement everything (along with going through considerable trial and error). By contrast, the more you can invest, the less of your time it will take to implement your marketing strategy.

For example, if your time is limited, you can focus on automated tasks and tests such as a search advertising campaign on Google with a limited daily and monthly budget. This means that you can set it up and forget about it for a month knowing that your budget has been set. While this isn't the best approach, it is an option if you know that you are unlikely to have the time or focus to review it each day or week.

Being clear on the amount of resources you are willing to make available upfront means that you'll be able to select techniques that suit your requirements and gives them the best chance of success. A common problem that I see is businesses underestimating the resources involved in different strategies and then abandoning that option when it gets too hard or they lose interest.

I've seen this most often with social media. A business may start a Facebook page because they think it's the 'right' thing to do and then after a month run out of content ideas and leave the page stuck in a time warp. Apart from being a waste of effort to set it up in the first place, it sends a poor message to customers. They may wonder if you're still in business. This approach should be avoided wherever possible. It is better to take the page down than leave a 'ghost' page with virtual tumbleweeds rolling through.

The key thing is to know what you can commit in terms of time, budget and staff, and then plan accordingly.

So how do you know what to commit? It comes down to measuring and testing, which I'll discuss in Chapters 7 and 8.

Sometimes business owners are reluctant to commit resources until they know what the likely payback period will be. In other words, they are happy to commit more money to marketing if they know that it will yield profitable results within three months.

However, until you've run tests to see which marketing channels work best for your business, you won't know this. An experienced marketer in your area may be able to make an educated guess, but it is still essentially unknown. Gathering this data is an important part of your market research and the right combination can become a competitive advantage for your business.

YOUR COMPETITION

It's also important to consider what your competitors are doing, as far as their marketing is concerned.

If the rest of your competition is doing everything one way, taking a different approach can provide extra cut through. One idea is trialing some offline marketing at a time when most small businesses are using digital mediums.

If you were marketing to a special interest group, for example, you could advertise in special interest magazines, speak at associations and run activities with user groups. If your target market isn't aware of your business, promoting a special offer with a flyer in a specialist magazine could be the best way to reach them.

The same goes for timing. If your competitors are aggressive and active, this may mean that you need to be more active to counter their message and position your offering as a viable alternative. You may decide to pick those platforms that your competition isn't using but would still allow you to reach your target market. If they're active on many different mediums then you may need to step up your activities on those platforms too and get smarter about the way you present your brand. Study what they're doing and consider how you can do it better. If your competition is a large business then look for opportunities that they're missing or sharpen your pitch to focus on a particular audience they're not addressing.

Depending on the size of your following, social media can be a great way to quickly get your message out to your market and to counter your competitor's message. If you have a sizable database then speaking directly to your customers through email marketing is another way to provide an alternative to your competitor's activities.

If you don't have a sizable social media following or a large database of customers to email but can see that this would be a good way to future-proof your business against your competition then being more active and offering valuable content will encourage more customers to connect with you.

SUMMARY

The type of marketing techniques you choose to implement will be influenced by a number of factors, including your target market, your product, your preferred level of involvement, your resources and your competition. By considering these factors before you commit to any platforms, you will be able to launch a sustainable marketing strategy to grow your business.

KEY ACTIONS

❖ Consider which marketing platforms would be best for your business, based on the following questions:
  - Who is your target market? Where are they most likely to see you?
  - How might your product influence your choice of platform?
  - What level of involvement would you like to have? Do you want to be hands-on or automate everything? How might this influence the platforms you choose or the schedule you work towards?
  - What resources do you have available? Are you prepared to spend more time or more money to get results?
  - What is your competition doing?

CHAPTER 7

MEASURE YOUR MARKETING

One of the benefits of online marketing is that every aspect is trackable—every click, open, download and form completion. This data provides clues of what's really going on with your business, clues that you can use to make improvements and get better results.

For example, you may notice an increase in your website visitors but no corresponding increase in sales. When you drill in to the details, it becomes obvious that there is also an increase in the rate of abandoned shopping carts, which indicates that although more people are coming to your site and adding products to their shopping carts, they aren't finishing their purchase. This indicates that there is a problem with your checkout process, which you can then address.

However, this also comes with its disadvantages, the key one being that you can end up with a lot of data, much of which isn't useful unless you know exactly what it means and what to do with it.

The key to understanding what is happening is to have an understanding of the key metrics for different activities. This chapter covers the key data you need to track to determine if your activities are yielding the results you want, including customer metrics, website metrics and marketing platform metrics.

Customer Metrics

Customer metrics measure the number and value of your customers. This information can help you to see what is working and what isn't. But more importantly it can help you work out your returns on your marketing expenditure.

Customer Counts

A key customer metric is customer counts or the number of orders that are received. How many customers did you have this week, month or year, and how does that compare to last year or quarter?

This metric is important because today's customers are tomorrow's sales. If customer counts are increasing, then you're heading in the right direction. If they are dropping off then you may not see a drop in revenue yet, but know that it will come. Monitoring this metric gives you an early warning that something is wrong and you may need to adjust some levers to get it back on track. Knowing this number also allows you to easily measure average spend per customer.

Average Customer Spend

This metric is one way of working out what a customer is worth to you over a twelve-month period and what the overall level of repeat business is.

For example, if you offer a product that retails for $49 and the average spend for each of your customers is $84, then you know that a percentage of customers order more than one product. If that number decreases on the rate for the previous year, then that would indicate that repeat business is falling away and you will need to investigate why that is happening. Perhaps you ran a number of promotions in the previous year and stopped because they weren't bringing in enough customers. By looking at the average spend per customer, you can now see that while the promotions weren't bringing in new customers they were encouraging existing customers to re-visit your site and make a purchase.

The formula to determine average customer spend over twelve months is:

Total Customer Spend for 12 Months ÷ Number of Customers =
Average Customer Spend

Lifetime Value of a Customer

The lifetime value of a customer is a prediction of the likely profit you would earn in your future relationship with a customer. This is important because it focuses on long-term relationships rather than short-term gains and provides a more accurate guide to what you can spend on customer acquisition and still maintain a profit.

It's also useful to know because it will help you determine the amount you should be investing in acquiring new customers. If a customer only ever makes a single purchase, then it doesn't make sense for there to be a high upfront investment in acquiring them. If your customers typically spend a lot more over time than they do on their initial purchases, then it makes sense to spend more to acquire them.

Let's say that you spend $25 to acquire each new customer and his or her first purchase is typically a $10 introductory product. From a straight accounting perspective, you've lost $15 on the sale of this product. However, because of the way your sales funnel is set up, you know that most customers go on to purchase the complete version of the product for $100 within six months. Over the course of six months, you have then made $85 on your customer (sales ($100 + $10)—acquisition expense ($25) = $85).

Going forward, they then usually spend $100 each month on new products with a fifty per cent margin. The monthly churn rate or the number of your total customers that drop off each month is five per cent.

($100 Monthly Revenue × 50% Gross Margin) ÷ 5% churn rate = $1,000

When weighed up against that initial acquisition cost of $25, $1,000 is a very good return.

To work out your customer's lifetime value, the formula is:

(Average Monthly Revenue per Customer x Gross Margin per Customer) ÷ Monthly Churn Rate = Customer Lifetime Value

The formula uses averages to smooth out the bumps of comparing individual customers, thereby making the measurement more meaningful across your business.

Once you've worked out what the lifetime value of a customer is, then you can use this information to figure out how to increase this.

The first thing to consider is what triggers variations. When has the average customer's lifetime value been higher or lower than it is now? Why was it different? Were you able to reduce the churn rate? Did you raise your prices or change your offering? Did you invest in a follow-up marketing strategy to turn more leads into long-term customers?

Making adjustments in these areas can have a big impact on your bottom line.

Another thing to consider is those customers who don't make repeat purchases—tracking the percentage of customers who don't purchase again within six months would be a good way to stay alert to any potential problems with your follow-up marketing.

WEBSITE METRICS

Website metrics measure how people interact with your website. This information can help you to determine how visitors are interacting with your site and where the problems are.

All of these metrics can be measured through Google Analytics, a free, online tool provided by Google. To set up the tracking a small piece of code needs to be inserted on every page of a website (typically it is added to a header or footer, as that applies to every page).

This reporting is comprehensive and allows users to drill into a variety of areas including visitor demographics, how visitors flow through your website, where they are located, what browser they use, and whether they are using a desktop, tablet or mobile to reach your site. For now, the most important metrics to focus on are your visitors, bounce rate, conversions, average spend per sale and abandoned cart rate.

Visitors

The first website metric is the number of visitors your website is getting over a given period. This comprises two metrics—the total number of visitors, and your number of unique visitors.

The total number of visitors, or views, is the total number of times that people visited your website over a given period. The key thing to keep in mind is that many of these visitors may not be unique visitors. This means that, rather than every visit, or view, being a new person, some visits were made by the same people returning to your website.

By contrast, the number of unique visitors is the number of different people visiting your website. So, if a visitor comes to your site once on Monday and again on Wednesday that will be recorded as two visitors, or views. However, because the same person visited twice, they are one unique visitor.

By comparing the number of unique visitors to the total number of visits to your website, you can get a sense of how often visitors tend to come back to your site and how engaging your content is. If the number of unique visitors is roughly the same as the total visitors coming to your site, that means you are getting very few repeat visits to your site. By contrast, if the number of unique visitors is very low in comparison to the total visitors coming to your site, this means you aren't getting many new visitors. The key is finding a balance between the two—you want former visitors to come back for more, but you also want a healthy stream of new visitors coming to your site.

This metric is also useful for measuring changes over time. If you've made a number of changes to your website, such as adding a blog and regularly publishing new content, and the number of unique visitors increased then that is positive. However, if the differential between total visitors and unique visitors increased further then the changes have worked to get more repeat visits.

Bounce Rate

Your website's bounce rate refers to the percentage of visitors who left your site without clicking on any links. They took a quick look, didn't find what they were looking for and left. Bounce rates vary depending on your site and your industry, and usually sit between twenty-five per cent and seventy per cent.

While comparing your site to the average is interesting, the real value is in comparing its performance on a monthly basis, particularly if you are making changes to the content or layout of your site. Have the changes made your site more enticing or less?

Bounce rates are measured for each page, which can help you assess which pages are giving your visitors what they want (because they have a low bounce rate) and which ones are not fulfilling their expectations (because they have a high bounce rate).

Average Time On Your Site

This metric is an indication of how engaging your content is. Perhaps you have a two-minute video on your home page but the majority of your visitors are only staying on that page for thirty seconds. This would indicate that your video is not compelling enough to make visitors want to watch it. Or it could be that there are too many other links taking visitors deeper into your site that are diverting their attention. To determine the real reason, you'd need to look at where they are going after they leave your home page. Are they leaving the site or clicking on a link? If its the latter perhaps it would be better to move the video to another page on your site or look at re-doing the video to make it more appealing.

This metric is also useful if most of your content is on a single page and there are few links for visitors to click on. Average time spent on the home page will be a better indication of engagement rather than the bounce rate.

Conversions

Conversions are one of the most important metrics that you can track. Your conversion rate is the number of sales or leads that you make as a percentage of unique visitors to your website.

The average website sales conversion rate is one per cent of unique visitors, or one out of every 100 visitors. The key with conversions is improving them, so if you double your conversion rate to two per cent then you can create twice as many sales without having to bring in more website traffic. This can have a dramatic impact on your bottom line, particularly if you paid to get those 100 visitors to your site through advertising or content marketing.

The process of improving your conversion rate is a growing area of business. Known as 'conversion optimization', it is a systematic approach of testing a number of variables in order to increase the number of converting visitors.

As well as fine-tuning your website, ensuring that you or your staff are not inadvertently impeding sales is a good idea. Some of the ways I've seen this happen are:

- No one has checked to see if the online contact us form is working properly—this is something that should be checked weekly or daily, depending on the volume of enquiries you typically receive.

- Speed of responding to queries—taking days to get back to a customer with a simple query is not helpful for customers.

- Not being clear about who is responsible for responding to queries received.

- When a potential customer makes an effort to phone your business, their query is not answered and instead they are referred to your website. Chances are they probably went to your website first and didn't find the answer they were looking for. In this more disconnected age, don't waste the opportunity to speak to a customer. It doesn't have to be an extensive chat, but a simple question like how they found your business after you've answered their query can be informative for customer service and product development.

There are a number of activities that you can undertake to increase your conversion rate, which I'll cover in Chapter 8.

Average Spend Per Sale

Average spend per sale is a key metric for businesses that sell more than one product. This metric is a reflection of how easy and appealing it is for your customers to add more products to their shopping carts as a result of cross selling and how easy it is to see what else you offer.

A key way to increase sales is to add the option to 'keep shopping' to your shopping cart. While it's important not to have too many distractions during the checkout process so that the customer completes the sale, offering the ability to quickly add more products seems like a no brainer (or at the very least, worth running a few tests to see if it is an option worth adding).

Abandoned Cart Rate

As I touched on earlier, there are a number of people who add products to their shopping cart but don't follow through and complete the sale.

Sometimes this can be because they want more information. Sometimes the shipping rate isn't clear and they want to see what the rate would be for their selected items. So the customer goes through a mock purchasing process to see how much it would cost to ship. Or maybe they want to see what difference a discount code would make to the price and whether it applies to the product they are ordering.

A website I visited recently didn't tell me whether the items I wanted could be shipped internationally until I had already added these items to my cart—a frustrating process for all parties involved.

As you can see, there can be many different reasons why this rate is high. The average for online retailers is around seventy per cent.

The good thing is that simply making information more accessible to customers before they check out can reduce this considerably.

PLATFORM METRICS

There are different metrics to track depending on whether you are marketing by email, on social media or advertising.

Email Marketing

There are two key metrics for email marketing—the open rate and click-through rate.

Your open rate is the percentage of people who open your email after receiving it. If you send an email to 100 people and ten people open it, then you have an open rate of ten per cent. An open rate of between twenty and thirty per cent is good, though you could get as high as fifty per cent if you have a small, responsive list.

The click-through rate is the number of times the website links in your email are clicked on. To continue the previous example, if two of the ten people who opened your email clicked on a link, then the click-through rate would be two per cent (calculated as the number of clicks divided by the number of people who received the email). The higher the click-through rate the better, as this indicates that your content resonates with your list.

Once you are aware of these metrics, you can then test how you can improve them. A common test is whether different days of the week or times of the day lead to better open and click-through rates. It used to be that Tuesday, Wednesday and Thursday in the morning were the best times to send emails, but with more companies doing this, you now risk becoming part of a tide of incoming mail. Similarly, Friday afternoons have traditionally not been seen as a good time, but I have seen positive results with this timing for some lists. Test and decide for yourself what works for your business and your customers.

Social Media

Each of the six top social media sites has slightly different metrics that you need to monitor to measure your impact. Followers, subscribers or page likes are figures that are often quoted and while it's good to know the overall number, it doesn't always measure ongoing engagement. What is more useful to track is the growth rate in the top number. Has the number of YouTube subscribers grown this month compared to last? Do you have more followers on Twitter this year than you did the previous year?

As I mentioned earlier, using a URL shortening service with social media saves valuable space and allows you to directly track the number of times a particular link has been clicked on, when it was clicked and whether any users have shared the link. It is useful to know this so you can see what is resonating with customers and which platform delivered the best response.

For Facebook and Instagram, the number of likes is often seen as a key metric. While this can be a guide to user interest, because it is so easy for a user to do, it isn't the best measure of how engaging your content is.

On Facebook a better measure is the number of times your content is shared, which is the online version of word of mouth. A share means that a user liked your content enough to proactively distribute it to everyone in his or her network. While still relatively easy to do, it does take more effort than a quick like.

On both Facebook and Instagram, the number of comments and interactions an update, video or piece of content receives can be a more telling measure for assessing how engaged your audience was with your post.

For Twitter, the number of followers is one measure that is easy to see at the top of each profile. However, to measure engagement other metrics to look at are the number of retweets (how many times others have shared your tweets) and how many times your posts have been favourited (the number of times your posts have been saved for later reference).

On LinkedIn the obvious metric is how many connections a person has. If it's over 500 then you'll only see 500+ and not the exact number. If you sell to other businesses and you're using LinkedIn to connect with potential customers then look for those that have over 150 connections as this indicates that they're active users. If not, you may go months without any response to your inmail or connection request. If you or your sales team has less than 150 connections then start getting active and demonstrate that you take the platform seriously.

If you are actively marketing on LinkedIn then the other metrics that are useful to view are the number of profile views you've received, how those people found your profile and your ranking compared to others with a similar background to you. This data can provide clues on how you're perceived, whether you're attracting people to view your profile that you're interested in connecting with and whether you need to be more active to make an impression.

On YouTube, you can review the number of subscribers to your channel, the number of views and likes or dislikes and comments. If you have a large number of views and likes but few subscribers then perhaps you don't have enough other content on your channel, don't update it frequently enough or you don't encourage viewers to subscribe in the text under your video.

When it comes to Pinterest, the key metric to look at is pins created from your website's content. If your content isn't being pinned as much as you'd like then you'll need to look at improving the quality of your images and your promotional activities. The other stat of interest is how often the content is being 'repinned' by others. This is the equivalent of shares on Facebook or retweets on Twitter and shows the level of engagement your pin is generating.

Advertising

When it comes to advertising there are two main measures that are important to track. The first is the click-through rate. Like with email marketing, this is a measure of the number of people who clicked on your ad compared to those who saw the ad. This rate varies depending on the type of ad, the location on the page, how well matched the content was to your target audience and how appealing your ad was to make users want to click to find out more.

The whole point of an advertisement is to generate an action. Sometimes it's to make a sale, particularly if you're primarily competing on price, but more often it's to start interacting with potential customers by them contacting your business by phone or email or signing up for your newsletter or to receive a special report. The more people that click on your ad, the more people that you have an opportunity to sell or engage with.

The other key metric is conversions. This is a measure of how many sales you make as a direct result of the ads you have running. This may be different to the overall conversion rate of your site, and ideally it should be higher because your ad is giving people a clear reason to go to your site, than them stumbling across your site through a search engine listing or content marketing.

For example, let's say that you're looking for a company to renovate your bathroom. You see an ad that promises to renovate your bathroom on time and on budget so you click on the ad. When you arrive at the bathroom renovation website, you are taken straight to a page that talks about the main problems clients encounter during their renovation and how a free report is available that discusses the top 5 tips to avoid these mistakes so that your bathroom is renovated on time and on budget. You want to find out more so you enter your name and email address. You have gone from an ad to a landing page and then to a page where you can download a report. The ad and landing page combination was successful at converting you into a lead and potential sale for this business.

When it comes to search engine advertising, another thing to measure is what your top keywords are. Which keywords have the highest conversions, and which just drive traffic that doesn't convert?

When it comes to banner ads, it's also important to measure which sites or placements have the highest conversion rates. Once you know which sites perform, you can then seek out similar sites with similar audiences.

CUSTOMER FEEDBACK

With so much of how we interact now digital and the general busy-ness of running a small company it can mean that you, as the owner, become removed from your customers' needs and their experience of dealing with your brand.

However, the truth is that if you're not getting repeat business, there are probably clues from your customers about why that is. Are there problems that they are telling you about, perhaps as a casual aside? These comments need to be recorded and tracked so that you can then run some tests and look for evidence to confirm whether what they are saying is true for all customers or a temporary glitch.

This is why it's important to get more qualitative feedback for your business, as this will tell you what to avoid and what you should do more of in future.

When did you last speak to a customer? If the answer is 'can't remember' then it's important to make connecting with customers a regular activity that you undertake. This could involve scheduling a time each week or month to phone several customers and chat with them.

Otherwise, one of the easiest ways to get feedback about your products, processes and new ideas is through online surveys. You can set up a survey for free with an online provider like Survey Monkey, which will create a unique survey link for you to send to your customers, and will collate the feedback for each of your questions.

TIPS:

- Have an introduction—Start your survey by explaining why you want feedback and what you're going to do about any input you get. If you've done a survey in the past, talk about the improvements that were made as a result of the input received, as this will encourage customers to respond again.

- Ask specific questions—Questions need to be based on what you want to know. Don't ask general or vague questions unless you are okay with general or vague responses. It's also a good idea to ask questions that let consumers answer in a way that doesn't make them feel like they are complaining or have unreasonably high standards. 'What is one thing we could have done to improve your experience?' is better than 'What could we do better to meet your expectations?'

- Time your surveys to suit your available resources— Take your customers' time seriously and only run a survey if you know that you'll be able to allocate resources to act on the feedback received and make improvements. This could be every three months or at two-year intervals.

- Get little bits of feedback often—You don't have to run a comprehensive survey to get feedback from customers. You could just ask one question after a transaction is complete. If you have a large number of transactions each day or each week, you can very quickly build statistically significant data. And by surveying customers who have just made a purchase, you are getting feedback from your hottest prospects rather than window shoppers. You can also quickly change what you're asking if you find you aren't getting useful information in return. Another option is to put together a survey to highlight one area that you know needs attention rather than a blanket 'how did we do?'

- Follow up on responses received—Show you're serious about taking action on feedback you receive by summarizing it and letting customers know what is being done to address concerns raised. This effectively continues the conversation and is likely to invite more dialogue.

- Recognize your brand champions—If people frequently respond and give you valuable feedback, recognize them by rewarding frequent contributors or awarding a prize for the best suggestion.

How Easy Is It to Contact Your Business?

The point of a survey is to open the lines of communication between your business and your customers, but you don't need to send your customers questions to get feedback. Make sure that in your daily operations you have a number of contact options available and that you respond to all queries received.

Being responsive towards your existing and potential customers is important because it demonstrates that you can listen to feedback, are responsive to their needs and are helpful and approachable. The result is that you're more likely to get their custom than a company that is unresponsive. This is because you've built up trust that you'll do what you say you will, you'll be more likely to provide support if something goes wrong and you are prepared to help them resolve questions they may have about your solution.

Some aspects to think about when reviewing your contact options include:

- Are you timely in responding to comments on social media? Ignoring your customers' comments, particularly complaints, leaves a vacuum that may well be filled by other disgruntled customers.
- Does the 'contact us' form on your website work? It is worth regularly checking this to make sure that it still functions correctly as the first sign of a problem is usually a lack of emails. If you receive ten email enquiries each day and suddenly none for a few days in a row then you'll know something probably isn't right. However, if enquiries are more infrequent then you may not know it's an issue until a customer complains or you realize after several weeks that it's been odd you haven't received any enquiries.
- Are your call center operators able to record and process feedback from customers? Does anyone look at it?
- Can feedback be sent via text?

Take It With a Grain of Salt

Although it's important to get to know what your customers want through surveys, sometimes, according to Steve Jobs, customers don't know what they want. While they may describe a problem, often there is a deeper issue at play.

For example, Jobs believed that people wanted a more responsive phone and was determined that his products would be stylus free. Yet before the iPhone was launched the Blackberry was ubiquitous, and featured a full QWERTY keyboard. As a result, there probably weren't many people asking for a touchscreen phone with a keypad built into the display. It wasn't until Apple created it that people realized that they wanted it.

So there is a balance between giving people what they want and surprising them by exceeding their expectations in a way they didn't expect but appreciate and value. Some questions to ask to determine if it is better to give people what they want or surprise them are:

- What is the underlying problem you are trying to solve?
- What customer feedback have you received? What is the real issue behind the feedback?
- What would be the best possible solution you could offer your customers? How can you provide that solution? Would it be cost-effective? If not, how could you provide the same result so that it was?

SUMMARY

The final step of any marketing campaign is measuring the response. Otherwise, how will you know whether it had any impact on your business? By measuring key metrics, you can see exactly what difference each marketing campaign made, which will show you what you should be doing more of, and where you shouldn't be spending time and resources.

The exact data you need for your business will vary depending on your business setup and the marketing activities you undertake. The key areas are customer metrics, website metrics, platform metrics, and customer feedback.

The benefit is that, once you have measured these areas, you can use this data to further optimize your marketing.

KEY ACTIONS

- ❖ Set up Google Analytics tracking on your website.
- ❖ Research different email marketing providers, like MailChimp and InfusionSoft.
- ❖ Review your current engagement levels on social media.
- ❖ Sign up for a free Survey Monkey account.

❖ Review the ways customers can contact you and how responsive
your business is.

CHAPTER 8

OPTIMISE YOUR MARKETING

N ow your marketing plan is up and running and you're measuring your results. So what do you do with all of this information? Optimize, of course!

Just as ongoing improvement is crucial to your product remaining relevant with your customers, you need to be prepared to continually tweak and update your marketing approach based on what's working and what isn't.

With the number of tools available today to measure your online marketing efforts, this is easily accessible for every small business.

WEBSITE OPTIMISATION

Split testing is a controlled way of testing different elements to find the approach that gets the best results. The simplest split test to do is a straight A/B test, where you measure the results of two different approaches to determine which performs best.

For example, you might create two versions of your homepage and divert half your website traffic to one page while the other half is diverted to the other page. You would then measure which homepage achieved the best results, based on your goal for that page. So if your goal for your homepage were for people to subscribe to your newsletter, the homepage that got the most subscribers would win. If your goal were for people to request a quote, the homepage that resulted in the most quote requests would win.

For this to work, it's important to keep in mind that you need a high volume of traffic to see a statistically significant result. I would look for a minimum of 1,000 visitors to each variation before deciding on a winning variant. If, however, you had 1,000 visitors to each page but very few took the action you were looking for or the results were relatively even then you would let the test run for another 1,000 views per variation.

Multivariate testing involves testing a number of different elements on one page at once. While this is a more thorough approach compared to a simple A/B test, the challenge is getting enough volume to be able to determine a result. The more variables that are being tested, the more traffic needed to get a statistically significant outcome. If 1,000 visitors is the minimum number that is needed per variation then if you are testing 5 different elements then it would seem that a total of 5,000 visitors are needed before you can determine which variation worked best. However, it is actually much more than that because a multivariate approach means testing each combination so the volume of traffic required is actually 25,000 visitors (5 variations x 5 combinations x 1,000 web visitors).

Once you have a winner, you can then continue to run smaller tests. So let's say that version A of your homepage results in twenty per cent more leads than version B. You can then set up another test using version A as the control (which would receive ninety per cent of all web traffic) while the remaining ten per cent of traffic is sent to a modified version of the page where you might tweak the headline, imagery or call to action. The aim is to find another version that can beat the original control version, which then becomes the new control.

While this may seem unduly tedious, small changes can result in a big difference to your bottom line, especially when you get a lot of traffic.

Split-testing Example

10,000 WEBSITE VISITORS

5,000 VISITORS (VERSION A)	5,000 VISITORS (VERSION B)
CONVERSION RATE 1.2%	CONVERSION RATE 1%
TOTAL SALES 60	TOTAL SALES 50
PROFIT $6,000	PROFIT $5,000

In the example above, let's say that over a one-week period your site receives 10,000 visitors. In the A/B test, that is 5,000 visitors to each page. Your former conversion rate for sales was one per cent, so for every 100 visitors you would get one sale. 10,000 visitors to the site would normally result in 100 sales.

However, version A achieved a twenty per cent increase over version B (your existing home page), which means that instead of fifty sales there were sixty sales. If each sale was worth $100 profit then this test yielded $1,000 more profit for version A.

Using version A as the new homepage without doing any other split-tests would mean your new conversion rate would be 1.2 per cent, or 120 sales for 10,000 visitors. That means an increase of twenty sales which equates to $2,000 extra profit.

As you can see, continually tweaking your website to make it better is a smart business move, and something that most leading companies do regularly. If there are websites of companies that you admire, Google 'Way Back Machine' to see how they have changed over the years.

SEARCH ENGINE OPTIMISATION

Split testing is one form of website optimization. The other is Search Engine Optimization (SEO) or the art of making your website rank higher in search engine results when potential customers search for keywords and phrases related to your business, product or service.

SEO works especially well if you've done search engine advertising and know exactly what your 'money' keywords are, or the keywords that result in conversions (sales or leads) on your website.

By making sure that you appear at the top of the search results (or on the first page) for those keywords you can potentially save on your advertising costs if a visitor clicks on your search engine listing rather than your paid ad. In addition, seeing your site come up twice, once in the paid section and the other below in the regular results, confirms that your site is able to offer what the visitor is looking for and crowds out the competition from a screen 'real estate' point of view.

So what can you do? There are two aspects to search engine optimization: on-page optimization and off-page optimization.

On-page optimization refers to all the things you can do on your website to improve the relevance and rankings of your site. This includes page titles, internal linking, regularly updated content (particularly on your home page), site load time, meta-tags and descriptions. Ensuring that you have content for each of the meta-tags is a basic first step as is relevant page titles. Internal linking and descriptions are a little more involved but using a platform like Wordpress makes this easier to implement.

Off-page optimization refers to activities that you can do on other websites to link back to your own site. This includes article marketing, social media, guest blog posts, directory listings and forum posts. The more links back to your own site, the more highly regarded your site is considered to be and the more credibility those sites have, the more credence is given to those links. So it's about volume of links and the quality of the sites linking to you. For example, a link from a major online news site carries more weight than a site with little content and a lot of links to other websites.

ADVERTISING OPTIMISATION

Just as you can split test elements on your website for higher performance, you can do the same with the copy and images in your ads. This is crucial to improving your return on investment and should be part of the way that you set up campaigns from the beginning. With split testing, it is best to trial different ads from the beginning of a campaign. Once you get a winner then you can tweak different elements of each ad to further improve performance.

The types of elements that you can test or review include:

- Headlines
- Ad copy
- Call to action
- Placement—where your ad appears on a page
- Size
- Location—which sites yield the best results?
- Keywords—which keywords have the highest conversions
- Time of day—are there times of the day that work better than others
- Landing page—improving the performance of the page where your traffic arrives after clicking your ad

Once you know what works you can then adjust your campaigns to replicate the results across other environments.

SOCIAL MEDIA OPTIMISATION

Social media can be a little more difficult to assess in terms of your return on investment as it's often more about keeping the lines of communication open between you and your customers as well as making it easy for them to share your content. This can make it harder to track the conversions that result from your social media activities.

However, you can assess your social media in terms of interactions versus effort. For example, if you devote considerable resources to Twitter but after six months your followers haven't increased dramatically and there is little interaction with those people in your target market then you're probably better off focusing on other platforms that do yield better results.

CONTENT OPTIMISATION

Once you've tried out a few things—blog posts, articles— and have tracking in place to measure their effectiveness, working out what is working and what isn't will become easier to decipher. It's then a matter of analyzing the activities that are appealing and trying to work out what resonated. Do they have anything in common? Is there a common theme, structure or style of writing?

It's just as important to look at those activities that didn't appeal and see if it's possible to pinpoint why they failed to gain traction. If it was a blog post, was the headline unappealing? Was the text difficult to read? Was the content inappropriate for your target market? All the different elements need to be assessed and compared to other blog posts that didn't get as much attention as expected to see if any patterns can be identified.

By paying attention to these insights you can:

- Increase your content's effectiveness to get maximum benefit,
- Gain important insights about what your customers value and what they are less interested in, which makes it easier to give them what they want,
- Use this knowledge to develop new content and products, and
- Gain a competitive edge over your less attentive competitors.

When evaluating the effectiveness of your content look for:

- What articles or blog posts attracted the highest number of page views in the past month?
- Which ones received the lowest number?
- Were any comments received directly below the article, via social media or through your contact form?
- What do the top articles or blog posts have in common? Were the headlines clear and engaging? Were they placed on high traffic sites? How long was the content? Did they attract the attention of high profile social media personalities?

- How can you replicate the features that made the top articles or blog posts successful?
- What can you learn from the content that received low interest?

SUMMARY

Innovation in marketing comes about by continually reviewing your activities to see what has worked and what hasn't and by adopting a testing mindset. By starting small, you can test what works and what doesn't before committing a larger budget to pursue success.

The big opportunities for optimizing your activities include website optimization, SEO, advertising optimization, social media optimization and content optimization.

KEY ACTIONS

❖ Website optimization
  - Consider running a simple A/B split-test on your home page
  - List out the key elements on your site and decide what to test first
❖ Search Engine optimization
  - Where do you rank in the search engines for your key search terms?
  - Check if your main pages have site titles, meta-data and descriptions.
  - Check how many external links you have from other websites*
  - Test the load speed of your website*

---

* See Resources section for details of sites and tools that can help determine this information.

❖ Advertising optimization
- Create alternate versions of any ads you have running to see if you can beat your current results
- Work out a schedule to test each of the other elements—placement, landing page, keywords, size, location, and time of day.

❖ Social media optimization
- Assess your progress on each of the social media sites you're active on compared to where you were at six months ago.

❖ Content optimization
- Follow the checklist for determining your best and least appealing content

PART 2
PUT YOUR PLAN TO WORK

CHAPTER 9

MAKE YOUR MARKETING
REPEATABLE & SCALABLE

I n Part 1 you laid the foundations for your marketing plan. You built your brand, identified your niche, created collateral, and started reaching out to your audience through different platforms. The next question is how can you maintain those activities to continue to reap the benefits?

One of the key differences between small businesses and larger companies, apart from the size of their budgets, is that large companies have processes and procedures for how things are done. While as a small business you don't want to become bogged down in policies, guidelines and manuals, processes are the key to establishing a repeatable and scalable marketing program.

Documented processes will enable your marketing plan to get implemented, whether you are there to oversee implementation or not. These processes should cover the content creation, scheduling and review for each of your marketing platforms, customer service, responding to problems and managing your customers' data.

In each of these areas, the key parts of your process include the description of the task, the steps required, the time frame or deadline and who is responsible for the task.

CREATE A MARKETING ACTION PLAN

Content Creation

One of the biggest challenges facing all businesses that want to communicate more with their customers is feeding the content furnace. What often happens is that a blog, for example, is begun with great enthusiasm and a rough idea of doing one post each week seems modest and doable. After all, how hard is it to write a 300-400-word post? But then a staff member is away and a supplier is late with stock needed for the Mothers' Day promotion you have planned and all thought of producing blog content has been left behind. When you do come back to it, a month has passed and you can't quite get started again.

One common mistake that I see small business owners make is underestimating the time it takes to produce quality content. A 400-word article can appear simple and straightforward once it's finished, but there is usually a lot of research and drafting that goes into that one finished piece. Unfortunately, this means they often overcommit and can't deliver.

Instead, it's important to recognize that producing marketing content takes time and to set aside the time to do it.

Regardless of whether you're creating content for a blog, a podcast, advertising or emails, having a content plan to mitigate day-to-day upheavals is a good idea. Your plan should include what information will be produced, when, where it will be distributed to and who will be responsible for it. If you would like help with this I have created a content template in Excel that you can download from my website. The details are located in the Resources section at the back of the book.

To use a fortnightly podcast as an example, you could line up a schedule for the next six months which would include when you're going to record the audio, the theme, what you're going to talk about, any guests to organize, and any post-production information like content that appears at the beginning and ending of the finalized material like your introductory or closing music or promotional material.

Tools to help:

- Inspiration scrapbook—a great idea is setting up a file or Evernote document that captures examples that you and your staff spot in your website surfing, retail experiences and online shopping purchases. This can help ensure your inspirational well never runs dry. These could include appealing headlines, articles, brochures, tweets, Facebook posts and more. Make it a habit to capture all these through links or screenshots and add them to a file for future reference. Next time inspiration is needed, this should be the first place to look for ideas.

- Video editing and recording—Camtasia is a recording and editing package for videos. It's relatively easy to use and has a free thirty-day trial that you can use to try it out. Another program that is good for screenshots is Screencast.

- Audio editing and recording—Audacity is a recording and editing tool, which is great to use if you want to take out your 'ahs', 'ums' and pauses so that everything sounds more streamlined.

Scheduling In Advance

If you're worried about falling behind on your content schedule, a great way to reduce this risk is by scheduling your content in advance. There is software available so you can do this automatically for social media and blog posts, while you can record videos and podcasts in advance and then have a marketing assistant or freelancer upload them according to your schedule (I'll discuss getting help in more detail in the next chapter).

Tools that can help:

- Social media scheduling—Social media management programs like Hootsuite make it easy to put your message on multiple platforms at once and to set up scheduled posts. For example, you could set up the next month of posts on Twitter, Facebook and Instagram at one time. The free version is sufficient for most small businesses but there is also a paid version on offer if you need it.

- Blog post scheduling—If you have a WordPress website and blog, there is a free plugin called 'Editorial Calendar' which gives you a calendar view of your upcoming posts. This is a great way to schedule your posts and see at a glance what you have coming up.

- Email scheduling—There are a number of different third-party providers you can pick from, all of which allow you to schedule emails in advance. Many also offer 'autoresponder' functionality, where you can program a series of emails that will be triggered following a certain event, such as a subscription or sale. This can help ensure you maintain regular communication with your market by reusing the emails you have already written, rather than constantly having to create new content.

Measuring and Review

Of course, a plan is only as good as the information that went into creating it, which is why it's important to regularly update it as you get feedback from the market on what is working and what isn't.

Regularly reviewing how your marketing activities are going—what's working, what isn't, what's taking up most of your and your staff's time, and what's yielding the best results—is an important activity which needs to be scheduled into your diary. A six monthly review of your overall plan is ideal as well as smaller reviews to make sure activities are on track and where problem areas can be identified and dealt with as quickly as possible.

One of the simplest ways to monitor the performance of your marketing is creating a marketing dashboard to record all of the relevant metrics in one place. Creating a marketing dashboard gives you an at-a-glance view of how your marketing is performing, including areas you can optimize to get even better results.

This doesn't have to be a difficult process. To quickly get a marketing dashboard up and running you have two options—creating your own dashboard in Excel and manually updating it as required, or using one of the many online dashboard tools that can be automatically updated. Ducksboard.com and Cyfe.com are two examples of services that allow you to create a dashboard that updates automatically for a minimal fee.

If you have your own IT resource then you could look at something a little more complex like a dashboard in Excel that automatically pulls your data into each field when you hit refresh. Of course, as with many things in life, it's better to have something that you can get going quickly without too much effort and refine over time than trying to implement a deluxe solution only to get overwhelmed and abandon the whole idea.

Sample Marketing Dashboard

Overall data	Month 1	Month 2	Month 3
Turnover (including % change)			
Profit (including % change)			
Website data			
Unique visitors vs. total visitors			
Bounce rate			
Conversion rate (overall)			
Abandoned cart rate			
Customer data			
Lifetime value of a customer			
Average spend per customer in 1 year			
Customer counts			
Average spend per sale			

Campaign metrics

Email data	Month 1	Month 2	Month 3
Open rate			
Click-through rate (CTR)			
Total subscribers (including % change)			
Unsubscribes			

Conversions			
Advertising data (for each advertising channel)			
CTR			
Conversions			
Top keywords			
Top websites			
Social media data (for each social media channel)			
Likes			
Follows (including % change)			
Shares			
Conversions			
Content marketing data			
Views			
Downloads			
Comments			
Conversions			

How frequently you update this information depends on factors like your budget spend and whether you're in a testing or optimization phase. If you don't have resources to make changes on a weekly basis, for instance, then getting a weekly dashboard view isn't going to be very useful.

Once you have the dashboard set up, the next thing is to make its production and distribution part of your business processes. You don't want to have to continually ask for them or realize that four months has passed and you haven't had an update. Instead, you want to have them delivered to you to remind you that it's time to check in.

Review checklist:

- Who is responsible for updating the marketing dashboard?
- How frequently will it be updated?
- Who receives them?
- When will they be discussed?
- How frequently will we review our marketing plan? Tools to help:
- Marketing dashboard—Just creating a dashboard in Excel is fine for most small businesses, otherwise tools like Ducksboard.com and Cyfe.com can be synced with your social media accounts and update automatically.
- Website tracking—Google Analytics is a free, online tool that measures all the key website activity you will want to monitor.
- Email marketing—All of the major email providers, like MailChimp, InfusionSoft and Aweber, offer reporting on the open and click-through rates of your emails.
- Social media—Some social platforms, like Facebook, have in-built analytics for business pages. Meanwhile scheduling tools like Hoostuite also provide analytics on how your posts perform.

SYSTEMISE YOUR CUSTOMER SERVICE

While it's important to have processes in place for your marketing, that work won't lead to new or repeat business unless it can be backed up by consistently strong customer service.

Customer service is important for building a relationship with your customers and making each interaction with them, whether online or offline, a satisfying experience. It's also the key to encouraging repeat business.

In many respects repeat business is the easiest sale you can make. If customers have already bought your product and are happy with it then they don't need to be convinced about why they should buy your solution over your competitors'. They don't need to read more about the benefits they can get because they are already experiencing them.

So how can you systematically improve your customer service, both online and offline? The key is making it easy and enjoyable to do business with you. Some ideas to achieve this online include:

- Ensure your contact page provides a confirmation for each message submitted—both an on-screen and an email confirmation. Also include contact details for the customer to follow up if they need to.
- Ensure your contact page has a physical address, phone number and the name of who is responsible for handling queries sent through the contact form.
- Make your shipping information readily available— what is the price and timing of different delivery options?
- Maintain an FAQ page that is regularly updated with common customer questions.
- Offer accurate, detailed product information—be as descriptive as possible about each product or service. If you want to keep the on page description minimal then provide more comprehensive information as a pop up.
- Allow opportunities for customer feedback on each product— this could be a star rating and comment system, social media links or both. This is going to be more and more important from a search engine point of view, but it's also something potential customers look for.
- Make it easy for them to buy—provide trust symbols (like a security or lock symbol, payment processor logos, details of

your guarantee) and secure landing pages to process payments, create a quick and simple checkout process, and give your customers the ability to create an account that will remember their information next time.

You can also improve your online customer service by getting feedback from customers around what they liked and didn't like about your online ordering process, the information you shared and so on.

Whether online or offline, communication is key to good customer service. This includes keeping them informed of the shipping process and any problems or delays with their order and quickly answering questions.

So how do you achieve this systematically? In this case, staff training and clear processes and guidelines around communication are clear. For example, start an Excel spreadsheet for capturing customer feedback so that it's all located in one place and not on multiple emails and scraps of paper. This makes it easier to see if there are any trends, if there is an opportunity to expand your product range or change the way you operate that will increase customer satisfaction. It also makes it easier if you want to follow up with customers and let them know about changes you've made based on their feedback.

Another suggestion is to create a flow chart for how prospective customers ideally move through your sales funnel. Provide the URLs for each point along the way if appropriate as well as links to the relevant collateral that they receive at each point. Make sure that staff are familiar with this so they can quickly determine where potential customers are in terms of their readiness to buy. For example, if you prefer that prospective customers have signed up for your email series before you spend time having a one-on-one conversation then your staff will be able to sign them up over the phone and then schedule a meeting for two weeks out knowing that the series of 4 emails will be delivered over the next ten days.

Encouraging Repeat Business

While repeat business should be a natural consequence of good customer service, actively encouraging repeat business will achieve even better results.

You could do this by offering a discount on the normal sales price, or a special offer where they get a valuable extra with their next purchase. (This is another reason why you need to know who your ideal customer is as I covered in Chapter 3. It would be difficult to work out what that extra should be if you don't know who your customers are and what they value.)

Another idea is offering gift vouchers for sale. This is a great way for your existing customers to share their enthusiasm for your products with their friends or family. It also helps generate repeat business if you offer a product or service that isn't something your existing customers are likely to buy regularly.

If you decide to make gift vouchers available, make sure that they are beautifully presented. You want the giver of the voucher to feel proud to give the recipient the voucher, and not have them apologizing for how it looks even though the product is great.

TIP:

If you offer a gift card, make sure you include clear instructions on how it works and how to redeem the voucher for both the purchaser and recipient. This could include showing screenshots of where to enter the code or an explanation of when to enter the code. For example, 'you will need to enter your code during order confirmation after you've entered your contact details'.

You could also establish a loyalty program where they can achieve special rewards and discounts by registering as a regular customer.

You can systematize this through your email marketing schedule by sharing special offers and discounts with past customers at certain times of the year, or by having emails that are automatically triggered once someone makes a certain number of purchases, spends a certain amount of money or reaches a certain number of points.

Following Up

You can improve your customer service, and even create more business, by following up with both potential customers and existing customers.

Following up with a potential customer can be the tipping point to get the sale. If they didn't get the information they needed then you can give them that information in their follow up, and you can also add this information to your website and other communication channels going forward to improve the buying experience for other customers. If they did get the information they needed but went with a competitor, then you can find out why they chose that competitor and what you could have done differently.

How do you do it? I've seen many different approaches to this. Some companies send an automated email (assuming a user has logged in to the website) to follow up and remind the customer that they still have products in their basket ready for checkout, or to ask why they didn't go ahead with the purchase. Others have a manual process where customer service staff personally call customers.

Whichever option you choose, to be effective you need to offer to help. As I mentioned above, it's important to find out why the sale didn't proceed. Was it just a lack of time or was there not enough information to make them enter their credit card details? Finding out what the reason is for customers abandoning their cart can have a big impact on your conversion rate.

If customers say that their main reason for not going ahead was the cost of shipping was considered too high, you could then make it a priority to negotiate a deal with a courier company to reduce your costs. If that, in turn, halved your abandoned cart rate from twenty per cent to ten per cent, this would have a significant impact on your sales and profit.

The other area where it's important to follow up is after a purchase. The benefits of following up after a successful purchase is that your customers are more likely to get better results with your product if they use the information you share, and they will also feel more cared for as a customer. This then makes them more likely to buy from you again.

One idea is creating a series of email messages that can enhance your customer's enjoyment of their new product. The type of information you might include could be:

- Information explaining how to get the most out of the product,
- Tips on how to use it,
- Other customers' experiences—this validates their decision to buy and also shares knowledge and fast-tracks their success, and
- A link to your FAQ page.

The email series can be scheduled to be sent on a set interval, for example, one message is sent one hour after purchase, a second a day later and a third one week later.

MANAGING CUSTOMER DATA

Of course you can't follow up with your customers and deliver excellent customer service if you don't know their details. One way to store and manage these is with a Customer Relationship Manager (CRM).

A CRM is a centralized system for storing client information. It can record information customers have supplied, like their name, location and birthday, along with metrics on their behavior such as purchase history, whether they open your emails and communication preferences, all of which make it easier to communicate with them in a targeted way.

For example, if a client is no longer active, you could then do some follow-up marketing with them after a year or so later to see if they are happy or if they would like to re-visit working together. A CRM could also allow you to set up automated messages to send a client useful information or payment reminders.

Beyond the ability to record customer information, a secondary benefit of having a centralized CRM is that if staff leave your business, then all the information on the clients they've been dealing with stays with the business and you can see where they are at with each client (assuming the information is being updated regularly). By contrast, without one, information about key clients tends to leave when staff do.

It also means that everyone can see what happened with a client, so if a key staff member isn't available when a client calls, other staff members can access their information to serve them effectively.

They also create a systemized way of gathering client information. Rather than relying on the memory of your staff, or having each person follow their own system, the input fields act as a reminder of what information is important to collect and monitor.

However, like anything, these systems only work if staff actually use them and update information when it changes. These systems can also be challenging to set up, depending on how many customers you have and the volume of information needed on each. It can be a process of trial and error to figure out which system is best for your business. That said, once you have set up your CRM, the benefits far outweigh the disadvantages.

Tools that can help:

- There are a number of different options when it comes to a CRM system. Salesforce is probably one of the better-known systems. Other options include CapsuleCRM, Zoho, Maximizer and Dynamics CRM. Costs and functionality vary for each and it's worth working out what you need and then investigating a few options before making your choice.

MANAGING PROBLEMS

Few small companies launch a marketing campaign in the hope of getting a negative reaction. But problems do happen. A seemingly innocuous blog post or social media comment can easily be misinterpreted and next thing you know you have a potential PR crisis on your hands.

Having a plan in place is important to ensure you can improve the situation, rather than making it worse. So what should you do?

Step 1: Don't panic

The last thing you want to do is overreact and close your social media account as that can look worse, like you have something to hide and are running from the problem. Take a breath and assume that what has happened isn't personal, even if it feels like you are the one being attacked. Misunderstandings can happen easily in a world where it's easy to shoot off comments behind the relative anonymity of a keyboard. View this situation as a problem to be solved, not abandoned.

Step 2: Apologize and acknowledge

Even if you aren't apologizing for a faulty product, you can say sorry for the problems someone is experiencing. A conciliatory, concerned tone is important for dispersing the tension and making them feel heard. Respond once or twice to answer combative answers.

If the tone in subsequent tweets or posts continues to be aggressive, then take the discussion offline as quickly as possible. If the person is a customer and you have their phone number, call them. If they aren't then try to get their email address so you can have a one-on-one discussion without the full glare of the internet watching and pitching in.

Step 3: Fix it

If the problem is a faulty product then do what you can to investigate and fix it. If the issue is a blog post that your customers object to then consider removing or amending it. If it's an advertisement that is causing offence, then pull it. The key is to take action to make amends.

Step 4: Feedback

Let your website visitors, customers or social media followers know what action you've taken to resolve the issue. Be as upfront as you can and invite other suggestions on how you can improve.

Yes, it may be uncomfortable, particularly if you get a flood of new comments, but here's the thing: those negative views are already out there and by bringing them to the surface you have a chance to be part of the conversation. By addressing them head on, you can take action and help your customers and your business to move on.

The problem with not addressing issues that arise is that it looks like you don't care about your customers' problems and are only interested in taking their money. This isn't a good look for any business. It may prompt not only those affected but anyone that sees it to look for alternative options.

For example, I recently saw a number of customer comments on a fashion company's Facebook page about problems many of them were experiencing trying to access the company website. There was no response from the company to these concerns and they have continued their posts and other marketing activities as if there is no issue. This is frustrating for customers as they feel that they are being ignored, they know from checking the Facebook feed that it isn't just a problem with their connection and they are trying to help by pointing out that they can't spend money with the company. Many customers will just give up and look elsewhere for what they want. If they still remain a follower on the page and an email subscriber, they are more likely to be skeptical that the company can be trusted.

It would have been better to acknowledge that there were problems with the site, explain what those problems were, hold off on further promotional activity and generally empathize with their customers' frustrations so that they feel heard and not ignored.

TIPS:

- If you're making changes to your product or how your customers use your product, then some problems can be avoided in the first place by taking customers on the journey when you implement those changes. Explain what you're doing and why it's happening and invite feedback. While that wouldn't cover everyone who interacts with your product, you may find that customers will jump to your defense if you've been upfront about what you're trying to do.

- Can playing along turn around the issue? This is a judgment call on how serious the issue is and depends on your ability to respond in a way that lets people know that what happened was silly and you're in on the joke. For example, there was a recent experience posted online that a user had with Amazon customer service. The customer was unhappy because tracking showed delivered but he hadn't received his book. The Amazon representative's name was Thor and the customer's first question was 'Greetings Thor, can I be Odin?'. A fun exchange played out that solved the problem but took any negative emotions out of the situation.

- Speed is crucial—if you can stem the tide before it spirals out of control then you have more chance of being able to limit the damage.
- Make sure it's clear who within your company is responsible for handling problems and when they should get you involved.

Tools that can help:

- If your business receives a lot of customer queries or needs to provide a help center then helpdesk software like Zendesk can make the management and delivery of this information much easier. Zendesk is a paid service based on the number of users who have access to the system. It is a better way to handle customer problems than emails or scrap paper as there are built-in follow-up processes. It is also relatively easy to set up a knowledge base to reduce customer problems.

Managing Internal Problems

Internal problems that become public and result in negative publicity often involve disgruntled former staff and others who have worked with your business. While they may or may not be publicly negative about your business, they can disrupt your systems and processes.

Social media shouldn't be the space for airing dissatisfaction and if the situation does arise where a former employee or connection is being negative towards your company, the key is having a process to take it offline as quickly as possible.

In one case, a conference company I once worked for had some negative feedback on social media about the lack of diversity in their speaker line-up. They were criticized for not having enough women on the agenda and for using black and white speaker photos to cover up the fact that most of the speakers were white males.

A couple of comments quickly became a cascade of negative posts. However, by going over the comments we saw that two people were driving the conversation. One was a member of a user group that the CEO knew, so he contacted her directly to discuss her concerns. The other had been to a previous event, which meant we had his contact information on file.

I gave him a call to chat to him about the issues he'd raised. He was a bit surprised at receiving a call and, while not initially receptive, after he had a chance to vent his frustration we were able to chat about why this situation had arisen.

I explained that the company had valid reasons for both issues. A number of women, in an industry dominated by men, had been invited to attend but due to a variety of reasons—time commitment required, family reasons, clashing timetable—only three females out of forty were able to accept. The photos were in black and white for purely aesthetic reasons. Speakers sent in their own photos, which were of varying quality. By making them all black and white, some of that variability was negated.

During our phone conversation I asked him for his ideas on how we could improve the situation. He made a number of suggestions, which we were able to implement. One of which involved adding a policy section to the company website which included a Q&A on diversity, explained our commitment to diversity and spelt out our anti-harassment policy for our events. Another suggestion was reaching out to key women leaders in the space to ask for speaker suggestions.

We followed up with an email to let him know that we took his concerns seriously and explained the actions we had taken to address them.

We also introduced a formal policy internally for handling any similar disputes, which we were able to use when another issue arose a year later. This subsequent issue was resolved with considerably less angst and greater speed.

Beyond having the right processes in place, there are some pre-emptive actions you can take to limit any potential damage from former employees. The main problems arise where a former staff member had access to your website login information or social media accounts. To address this, their access needs to be revoked or the login details need to be changed.

TIPS:

- Remove the login privileges for former staff. If they have their own custom login details and you feel there may be a problem, change all your login information for the backend of your website, social media accounts, Google Analytics, email marketing, freelance account details and so on.

- Have all your marketing login information stored in one central location—while this can make it easier for a departing employee to copy, it is also easier to change because you can use the list as a checklist for what needs to be amended. It is also the fastest way of letting everyone in the business know what the new information is.

- Make sure that as the business owner you also have primary login information for your social media accounts and that it isn't just the person within your organization who set them up.

SUMMARY

The key to making marketing repeatable and scalable is to ensure you and your team have clear systems and processes, and then to support these with the many tools that are available for small businesses.

The processes to look at are a marketing action plan for creating, scheduling and measuring your marketing; customer service;

customer data management; and risk management plans for dealing with PR problems.

KEY ACTIONS

❖ Think about the different processes you could create to make your marketing more sustainable, including a marketing plan, customer service processes, customer details management, and processes to manage problems. Either draft the relevant processes, or engage someone to draft them for you.

❖ Investigate some of the different tools that could help with your marketing.

CHAPTER 10

GET THE HELP
YOU NEED

I f you have had marketing on your plate for a while and just haven't been making progress, then you've probably realized that this isn't the most effective strategy. Or perhaps you have tried using a mix of outsourcing and part-time staff to implement your marketing activities, only to realize that some things aren't being done. Ultimately, your marketing strategy to date has been a little haphazard.

If you're ready for a more cohesive approach, then it's time to raise the white flag and get some assistance.

However, knowing you need marketing help is one thing. Knowing what sort of help you need and how to get it is another matter altogether. Sorting through all the options and working out what is right for your business can be a confusing process, especially when there is always someone trying to sell you something (whether it's what you really need or not).

Without some knowledge of marketing it can be difficult to work out what you need, what is just a 'nice to have', what can wait and what is unnecessary for your business right now.

The different types of marketing help available include outsourcing, hiring new team members, or a mix of the two.

OUTSOURCING OPTIONS

Your outsourcing options include hiring freelancers for specific jobs or tasks, using an agency to plan, coordinate and implement a strategy, and hiring an online contractor to work on your business.

Hiring Freelancers

Freelancers sell their services at an hourly or project rate, which means you have the opportunity to work with experts in various fields without having to spend the time and money required to find a permanent employee.

The advantages of working with freelancers include:

- The costs can be a lot lower. First, you are only hiring someone to complete a specific piece of work rather than giving him or her a permanent salary, which is more cost effective. Second, due to online freelancing communities, you may be able to find someone overseas who is happy to work for a lower hourly rate.
- You're only hiring what you need. This lowers your risk, as you can always stop working with them if they can't perform the duties you need. It also gives you the opportunity to find freelancers who meet your requirements, who you can then call on repeatedly.
- This is a good way to test out a supplier before committing to using them on a more consistent or ongoing basis.

However, there are some disadvantages to hiring freelancers. These include:

- Depending on where they are based, time differences can make communication frustrating and slow down the workflow, especially when you need changes made.
- Communication is usually done via email or messaging and sometimes you just want to discuss the project to be clear that they understand exactly what you require.
- You may need to search through hundreds of freelancers to find what you want—either through the applications if you post a brief, or through the listed profiles to find a match.
- The success of the project often depends on your ability to clearly and succinctly explain what you need done—it can take time to hone this skill and get it right without lots of back and forth.

If you think freelancing might be right for you, where do you start? There are a lot of different freelancing websites around but the two largest are:

- Upwork.com
- Freelancer.com

Each of the sites has skilled freelancers registered from all over the world who can perform a variety of tasks, including marketing.

There are also a number of specialist freelancing websites that are more task-specific. 99designs.com, for example, offers graphic design services, from logos to book covers to t-shirts and websites. Meanwhile Textbroker.com and CrowdContent.com both focus on content writing skills.

With each of the sites you will need to join, at no cost, to interact with freelancers. Once you've signed up, you can either search through the freelancer profiles to find individuals with the skills and experience you're looking for, or post a project. If you post a project, once it's published interested freelancers will apply for the position.

Because 99designs.com is design focused, when you post a project, interested designers will submit designs for you to choose from. In other words, they mock up the project you've requested, which gives you the opportunity to see their ideas before you commit to a designer. Typically the higher the budget for your project the more designers you'll attract as they'll know that you're not a tire kicker and deserve to be taken seriously. The good thing is that if you don't like any of the designs then you don't pay.

Keep in mind that not all of the freelancers on these sites operate independently—some are part of an agency. If you specifically don't want to work with agencies, then you're best to state this up front so you'll have fewer applications to sort through.

TIPS:

- Don't assume anything—ask for more information up front than you would with a normal employee.
- Be clear about your expectations and what you want and don't want while also staying open to new ideas and possibilities.
- Make sure you have provided background information on your business—what you do, the products you offer and your brand.

Using Marketing Agencies

Many companies choose to work with a marketing agency that offers a range of skills and can therefore be a one-stop shop to meet your marketing needs. They will often have their own graphic designer to handle your visual projects, a web designer to take care of your website and technical projects, a copywriter to take care of your content, and expertise in PR, digital and offline marketing.

The advantages of working with a marketing agency include:

- You get access to a range of skills and experience that you can call on as and when you need to.
- You can get a mix of senior advice and juniors to implement.
- You can get access to experienced marketers and may be able to develop a relationship with the owners of the agency, depending on the size of the agency and the size of their typical clients.

The disadvantages of working with an agency may include:

- You can feel like you're locked in to the staff that the agency has available, which can make it difficult to pick and choose the skills that you want.
- As one of many clients that the agency deals with and, although you may have an account manager, you might feel that your business doesn't get the attention and energy that it needs.
- Staff turnover, particularly at the junior or mid-level, can be high, which means that your account is continually being handed from one person to the next.
- You may have little input from senior marketers or agency owners and feel like your business is overlooked, particularly if the agency specializes in medium to larger businesses and your firm is one of their smaller accounts.
- The turnaround time of the agency may not match what you need—they may not understand the urgency of a project, someone might be away, or there may be no clear escalation process.

- You're unlikely to get any training from the agency for your staff, as this means that you won't need their services anymore.
- If they operate on an hourly rate then there is little incentive for them to complete work quickly, and they may stretch the work or project as long as possible as it's in their best interests to do so.
- Having to relay the changes you'd like through an account manager can be tedious, and can result in the message getting lost in translation.
- If you decide to change agencies then you lose all the experience, background knowledge and metrics of what worked for your company and what didn't.

TIPS:

- Ensure that you understand who will be doing the work on your account and what services they can provide.
- Check whether you can deal directly with the agency's staff to access their expertise or whether it all needs to flow through the account manager.
- Some agencies specialize only in digital marketing or social media. If you want to have a one stop shop, it's better to get a single agency that offers a full range of services as you don't want to be limited to what they offer. (This doesn't apply if you have created your own marketing plan and know exactly what you want and how you're going to pull the different elements together.)

Hiring Online Contractors

Rather than hiring a freelancer to perform a specific task, you can hire a virtual marketing resource that works with your business on an ongoing basis. This could either mean employing someone offshore or someone who prefers, for family, geographic or lifestyle reasons, to work remotely.

The advantages of this arrangement include:

- Offshore staff can lead to considerable cost savings. As a result, you may be able to hire more than one resource.
- You don't need to increase your full-time employee head count and have all the associated costs and HR issues.

The disadvantages of this arrangement may include:

- Because the level of expertise varies considerably with offshore staff, you may need to offer more training than is needed for an onshore resource. Their level of output may also be lower.
- Language barriers can lead to frustrating misunderstandings that waste time and resources.
- They will need to be managed closely, especially in the beginning, to ensure work and output expectations are firmly established.
- It's important that the staff you hire feel engaged with the business and motivated to do their best work. This can be more difficult to achieve with remote staff members.

The key to making this type of arrangement work is having regular reporting procedures so you know what is being worked on, any problems they have encountered and what assistance they need to solve them.

The other part of the equation is keeping them up to speed with what is going on in the business to avoid them feeling like they are being ignored and 'the last to know' about any changes. This can be difficult if your business moves quickly and providing updates becomes another ongoing item on your to-do list.

TIPS:

- Request regular updates about what they are working on, any problems they are having and anything they need help with.
- Be clear about your expectations of their availability and whether they will be working during your regular office hours.
- Set up regular Skype chats so you can establish a level of understanding and rapport—this will be invaluable if problems arise.

IN-HOUSE MARKETING RESOURCES

If you aren't keen on outsourcing your marketing, in-house options include:

- Hiring a part-time or full-time employee. This could be hiring someone on a permanent part-time basis or splitting the role of an existing staff member so that marketing is part of his or her responsibility.
- Getting a contractor to come in each week to coordinate your marketing activities and do what needs to be done.

Hiring Permanent Staff

If you are considering hiring permanent marketing staff, the first thing you'll need to consider is their seniority. Do you want a marketing manager, or a junior?

Hiring an in-house marketing manager, although a considerable commitment maybe a good option for your business depending on your size and growth plans. If you turnover more than $5 million per annum and expect to grow quickly then hiring an experienced marketing manager is likely to be a good long-term investment.

As a general rule, the more experience they have, the more you can expect to pay. If you hire a marketing manager with considerable experience, it's also important to keep in mind that they will probably have been managing a team of marketing staff, have access to marketing systems and have an allocated budget in their current role and are likely to expect the same level of support in working for you.

If your turnover is between $5-10 million then having your own in-house marketing manager with a support team (either contractors or employees) and budget allocation makes sense. If your turnover is less than that you will need to carefully consider if that's the best use of your resources.

However, you may be able to find an experienced marketing manager on a part-time basis, which will help you leverage their experience at a lower expense.

If your turnover is less than $5 million then it probably isn't big enough to support an entire marketing team unless you have aggressive growth plans.

Another solution is to hire a marketing junior. As well as being a lower cost option, this can work well longer term for the business because the person can grow in the role, as the business expands, to become the marketing manager. As well as having someone that knows your business well, it also provides job advancement potential for an ambitious junior. To make the most of this arrangement, the marketing junior will need support from experienced marketers to learn, grow and remain motivated.

Whether you hire a manager or junior, the advantages of having someone in-house include:

- They will get to know your business well, which means you'll have a more consistent approach. This will also empower them to create more proactive marketing strategies.
- They are in your office so you can be more spontaneous, dynamic and interactive with them.

- They can react faster to issues that arise.
- You can develop your own in-house marketing resources, reducing your reliance on agencies and freelancers.

However, there are some disadvantages, including:

- If your staff member leaves then it will have a bigger impact on your business than if a freelancer leaves, as there may be no one else in the business who really knows what they did or how 'marketing' works. I've seen this often where the marketing manager has left and all the Intellectual Property around the business's marketing has left with them. Many small businesses don't have processes in place to capture information in a central, easily accessible location.
- There is less scope to adjust your needs based on the business performance as you've made a commitment to hiring an employee.
- The staff member you hire may not have experience across all platforms and tactics that the business needs.
- If you hire a marketing junior, then they may not have enough experience to be able to design a marketing plan and implement it without training and guidance.

TIPS:
- Be sure that this is the route you want to take before investing time and money in hiring someone on a permanent basis.
- Plan to provide training and support, particularly for a staff member with only a few years of experience.
- Make establishing a centralized marketing resource online where all important marketing information can be found a priority. This could include information like login details

for different sites, graphic files and imagery used in your collateral, a style guide and any formal plans (strategic, action, content, budget and more) that you have.

Engaging a Contractor On Regular Basis

This can work well if you would rather not commit to hiring a new staff member but want the consistency that comes from having the same person in your office each week or fortnight.

The advantages of engaging a regular contractor include:

- A contractor may be more likely to have the mix of strategic and tactical skills that you need, unlike a permanent marketing manager or junior. This is because they've often had to provide a range of services for different businesses in various industries.
- You can get the help you need when you need it.
- Depending on their availability, you may be able to quickly scale up or down depending on what needs attention.

The disadvantages of engaging a contractor include:

- They will likely still depend on you to set the agenda and decide on priorities, such as budgets and resourcing.
- They will probably have other clients or commitments and they may leave to take up a more permanent role if they are just contracting until something better comes along.
- They may be reluctant or unable to undertake work outside their set days.
- If they leave then you will be left without anyone to follow through on your marketing activities.

- There is usually a minimal notice period required from contractors—this works both ways, of course, as you can also reduce their hours as and when you need.

TIPS:

- Have regular briefing sessions with your marketing contractor so that they are up-to-date with what is happening in your business. This is particularly important if they come into your office once per week or less frequently.
- Have the contractor come into your office at least once a fortnight. Any less frequently than that and it may be difficult for them to maintain momentum with their marketing activities.
- Include the marketing contractor in decision-making and they will feel more like part of the team, which will make them more loyal to your business.

Mixing Outsourcing And In-House Resourcing

There is also an option to use both external and internal resources.

The advantages of this arrangement include:

- You can get the right mix of skills that you need for your business.
- This approach can be scaled up as required.
- You will spread the knowledge of your business rather than just having it reside with one person.
- You, as the business owner, will not need to be as closely involved in training the staff you hire.
- You will be able to offer customized training for your staff that is specific to what you need, which will allow them to implement

what they've learned rather than going off to do a course and then wondering how to make it happen in your business.

- It makes marketing more dependable as it is repeatable and scalable, which then enables growth for the future.

The disadvantages of mixing internal and external resources include:

- Finding the right resources—in a consultant/junior setup you would need to find a consultant who is both agreeable and able to take on a coaching and training role with your staff.
- This can be a more expensive approach, though it will likely have more benefits in the longer term.
- You will need to commit to this strategy for twelve to eighteen months to be able to assess whether it is working for your business.

How you decide to set this up will depend on your preference for the outsourcing and in-house scenarios outlined earlier in this chapter.

One example is hiring an experienced marketing manager who manages marketing strategy and outsources the day-to-day tasks like social media updates.

Another option is using a consultant to provide you with a plan and working with your own internal marketing staff to oversee implementation, undertake training as required, and provide a bigger picture approach. This can be a good option if you've hired a marketing junior. And if you take this approach then you will be building up your internal marketing expertise while still having an experienced marketer to set strategy and use as a sounding board as required.

WHAT'S RIGHT FOR YOUR BUSINESS?

Having knowledge of the various types of help that are available and the pros and cons of each is a good place to start. What you pick will depend on the size of your business, the resources available, how involved you want to be and whether you're looking for a short-term fix or longer-term solution.

The following table is a rough guide to what will work best for your business. Other factors that will have an impact on your marketing choices are your product, target market, competition and how aggressive you want to be with your marketing.

Turnover	Budget available	Your level of involvement	Goal	Type	Best option
< $1 million	Low	High	Short-term fix	Outsource	Hire freelancers for specific jobs
	Moderate	Medium	Short-term fix	Outsource	Contractor that works on ongoing basis
	High	Medium	Short-term fix	Outsource	Marketing Agency with specific skills

Turnover	Budget available	Your level of involvement	Goal	Type	Best option
$1-5 million	Low	High	Short-term fix	Outsource	Online contractors
	Moderate/High	Low	Long-term solution	Mix	Strategic consultant\ trainer + junior marketer
	Moderate/High	Medium	Medium-term option	Mix	Part-time employee + internal contractor
	High	Low	Short-term fix	Outsource	Marketing Agency (one stop shop)
	High	Low	Medium-term option	Mix	Marketing Manager + contractors
	High	Low	Long-term solution	Internal	Marketing Manager + junior
$5-10 million	Moderate/High	Low	Long-term solution	Internal	Marketing manager + team of 2-4
	High	Low	Long-term option	Mix	Marketing manager + Marketing agency + team of 1-2

	Outsourced Marketing Resources			Internal Marketing resources		Blend of Outsourced & Internal resources
	Freelancers	Marketing agencies	Online contractor	Permanent staff	Engaging a contractor	
Cost	$	$$$$$	$$	$$$$$	$$$	$$$$
Speed of service	««««	«««	««««	«««««	«««	«««««
Level of expertise	?	«««««	««	«««««	««««	«««««
Reliability	?	«««	««	«««««	««««	«««««
Control	«	««««	«««	««««««	«««««	««««««
Strategic alignment	«	«««	«	«««««	«	«««««
Sustain-ability	«	«««	«««	«««««	«««	«««««

SUMMARY

The key to deciding whether to outsource help, hire your own staff or a combination of both requires a review of your business needs and your turnover, level of involvement and timeframe for achieving results. The setup you decide on may change in the future as you grow. For example, you may start off hiring a full-time employee and as sales grow decide to outsource particular aspects of your marketing before expanding to two full-time staff.

KEY ACTIONS

❖ Review the chart outlining different approaches you can take with your marketing setup and determine where your business sits in terms of turnover and your desired level of involvement.

❖ Decide whether you're looking for a short or long term fix by considering other factors like your product, degree of difficulty in reaching your target market, competition, and how aggressive you want to be.

CHAPTER 11

QUESTIONS TO FIND THE RIGHT HELP

P icking a freelancer, contractor, consultant, employee or agency can be a challenge, especially when they could have a very large impact on your brand and how your target market perceives it.

This is why it's important to find the right person. To do so, you'll need to consider both what your business needs and what each candidate can offer.

QUESTIONS TO ASK YOURSELF

Before we get into what you should consider when looking for help, there are a couple of issues that you need to decide on first.

The first is knowing your marketing goals, both your short-term goals and your long-term ones as we discussed in Chapter 1. Balancing long-term and short-term needs is a constant challenge for many small businesses. You'd like the Rolls Royce solution but the budget won't allow it. Or you're so used to making do with duct tape and twine that you can't get your head around having the scope to sit back, breathe and plan a better way.

Even if you aren't sure exactly what you need, it's still a good idea to rough out some top-level objectives before talking to anyone. A goal could be increasing the percentage of repeat business or increasing sales for this year compared to last year. This will impact your hiring or outsourcing choice, from the type of help you choose to the number of people you bring on and how long you choose to work with them.

The second is deciding what you should outsource and what tasks would be better done in-house. In part, the answer to this question comes back to Chapter 6, which raised the question of how involved you want to be in marketing activities. Different options will have varied implications for you in terms of management time and input. Do you want to have someone in your office who you can chat with when inspiration strikes? Or would you rather it was all done elsewhere and you were updated as required? The other key consideration is what you consider to be business critical. If you want social media to be your primary method of communicating with your customers about product changes and this involves giving daily photo updates on what's new then having that function in-house makes more sense both in terms of organizing logistics and generating content ideas.

Once you have decided on these two areas, you can then start to look for the help you need.

WHAT TO LOOK FOR IN A CANDIDATE

Even if you typically hire based on your gut feeling, it is still wise to use a number of factors to formulate a shortlist. Some aspects to consider include experience, whether they can give you any recommendations or feedback, and their motivation for working for you.

Experience

What work have the candidates done before?

Many businesses look for marketing expertise in their particular industry as a starting point on the sorting process, often in the belief that the need to understand the peculiarities of an industry is crucial. However, marketing is about connecting with customers and building trust, which is relevant to every industry. Therefore a marketer's field of experience is less important.

While experience in your industry is not essential to be able to market products in that industry, what is important is to be able to demonstrate flexibility across a range of sectors. If a marketing professional or agency only has experience in dealing with heavy industrial companies, then handling a surf-oriented retail brand is going to be a challenge. This is not only because the two industries are vastly different but because they will likely involve different marketing techniques. Heavy industrial marketing is more about developing brand-building collateral, making personal business connections and changing perceptions at a business level compared to marketing a consumer brand like surf wear, which is likely to involve being in touch with a younger, savvy demographic through social media and recruiting brand ambassadors who resonate with the target market.

Beyond industry experience, the other thing to consider is the typical size of their clients. If a candidate is used to dealing with medium to large corporates then they are going to have a different approach to budgets, return on investment and branding. Larger companies will often have the budget to do more brand awareness activities whereas smaller companies are more focused on return on investment.

The other difference is the number of market segments that a business can pursue. A larger business with multiple divisions is able to allocate resources to several customer segments at once whereas smaller businesses can't afford to dilute their focus or they won't get enough traction in one to be able to fund the next.

Because of this, it's a good idea to choose someone who has demonstrated experience working with small businesses.

Recommendations

What recommendations or feedback do they have from existing or previous clients? This can be quite telling and often what is not said can be more revealing that what is. Did they exceed the expectations of their clients or give them exactly what they asked for? As a small business owner without a strong interest or detailed knowledge of marketing, you're unlikely to know all of the possibilities that marketing can deliver and you want people who give you more than you think is possible.

It's also worth asking if other business owners can recommend anyone for you to work with. Asking around can be a good source of information (assuming the business owners you ask have similar needs to yours) and is a common way for agencies, freelancers and consultants to get future roles.

Motivation

Why do they want to work for your company? Are they chasing awards or publicity, or do they want to give your business the best returns?

This is probably more applicable when it comes to dealing with agencies and can be assessed by listening to how they talk about other clients. Do they focus on the return on investment they delivered or about how great the imagery was or how clever an ad campaign was? Clever or pretty doesn't necessarily get you more customers, but it can win industry awards or recognition.

How Do They Market Themselves?

Finally, think about how they have marketed themselves or their business. While referrals or recommendations are a good sign of a proficient marketer, it's also important that they have been able to generate business through their own marketing activities. After all if they can't actively generate new customers for their own business, then how will they do that for yours?

HOW TO ASSESS THEIR MARKETING MATERIAL

Depending on where you find your marketers, there will be different factors to consider when assessing how they have presented themselves.

When you are reviewing applications and profiles on an outsourcing site, look out for the following:

- What experience do they have doing the kind of work you're after?
- How much have they earned as a freelancer through the site? (Many will have profiles on several different sites and work obtained independently so this is not necessarily indicative of their average earnings, but does give you a feel for the average dollar value of the projects they undertake.)
- How have they answered your brief—does it sound like they have a solid grasp of what's required?
- Have they provided samples of their work?
- What ratings have they received for the other jobs they've done?
- What qualifications do they have?
- If you're recruiting someone to write for you, then make sure that the answer to your brief is well written. Ensure they have submitted a tailored cover letter as part of their proposal, as their resume or work summary may have been written and polished by a professional writer.

When looking at a company or consultant's website there are a number of points to consider. I have come across many marketing companies with very slick websites that are more about style than substance and I've seen the other extreme where websites are substandard. There are other sites that only talk about themselves and not so much about how that relates to their customers. While the marketing company that you hire doesn't need to have the best looking website around, the site does need to address the following key points:

- A clear picture of who runs the company,
- What they can offer you,
- What they've done for other clients—there should be testimonials and case studies,
- How you can get in touch.

When looking at a potential employee or consultant's LinkedIn profile, you should feel comfortable that you're dealing with someone with both expertise and credibility. At a minimum their profile should have:

- A clear photo that shows their face,
- A detailed explanation of their roles rather than just a list and dates, and
- Qualifications.

Factors that are not essential but are nice to have include:

- Recommendations from clients and colleagues, and
- Articles they've published.

QUESTIONS TO ASK IN INTERVIEWS

In all interviews, the general questions you should ask include:

- What experience do you have?
- Can you provide examples of similar work you've done?
- What were the results?
- Can you provide references, client feedback or testimonials?
- What are three changes that you would implement to improve sales for my business?

On top of these general questions, there are also a number of specific questions you should ask each person you interview, depending on whether they are a freelancer, agency, potential employee, or consultant. For freelancers, ask the following:

- How do you decide what to work on and how to do it?
- On previous jobs did you do all the work yourself or did you have help?
- What is your timeframe for doing this work?
- What sort of work do you most enjoy—tactical, strategic, research, reporting? (You want to make sure that you're asking them to do work that they most enjoy doing so they are motivated and experienced.)
- How do you normally communicate with clients? Is it mainly by email or can you talk on the phone or video chat if required?

When interviewing agencies, ask:

- Who in your agency will do the work?
- Will I have an account manager? How will it work?

- What can I do if I'm not happy with how the work is progressing?
- What sort of reporting can I expect? What will it look like?
- How does your billing work?
- What size companies do you normally deal with?
- How long do most clients stay with you?
- What do you think is the best way for small businesses like mine to get more customers?
- How do you normally report on progress?
- How is information on clients shared within the agency?
- How is staff allocated to different accounts?

For online contractors, ensure you ask the following:

- Which hours will you be available to work?
- Which time zone are you in?
- How often will you update me on your progress?
- How do you handle problems?
- How can I contact you if I want to discuss something?
- Do you have other clients? How do you manage your workflow?
- What is your access to services like? Do you frequently have power or internet outages?
- How is your home office setup? Do you have your own computer in a dedicated office?

When interviewing a potential full-time or part-time employee, ask:

- What areas of marketing are you experienced in?
- How do you keep your skills up-to-date?
- How big is the marketing area where you're currently working?
- What was your role?

- Do you have experience managing freelancers or contractors?
- How do you decide what areas to focus on?
- How do you go about making changes?
- Have you ever implemented marketing systems and processes before?

When interviewing internal contractors, ask:

- When you go into a business how do you decide what to work on? (You want to find out if they will wait to be told what to do or will use their own initiative.)
- How do you usually work?
- What sort of work do you most like doing?
- Do you provide similar services to other clients?
- How do you keep track of what is happening in each business that you help?

Finally, when considering marketing consultants, ask the following:

- How have you come up with a strategic plan for a business that you've worked for? What do you base the plan on?
- How do you normally work with clients?
- What size clients do you normally deal with?
- Do you undertake training for a client's staff?

THE NEXT STEP

Okay, so let's say you've now done a series of interviews with a range of service providers and potential employees. What happens next?

It's time to make a decision. After coming up with a shortlist you may still struggle to decide on the best approach. If so, go through the following set of questions and see if you can further reduce your shortlist down to one.

Questions to narrow your shortlist:

- What assumptions am I making about how this relationship will work? Do I need to verify any of these assumptions with the candidates to ensure that I'm getting what I want?
- Am I being seduced by the latest tool or is it really what the business needs to grow sales?
- The presentation was impressive but what am I really getting? Will it help my business grow?
- Have they earned the right to provide the service they are offering?
- Does the solution capture the essence of my business and take me where I want to go?
- What is the expected return on investment? Have I set clear measures of what I expect?
- Did they ask good questions about the business? Did they make me think or just tell me what I want to hear?

It can be too easy to hand over authority if it's an area you don't understand. Instead of handing over the keys to the growth of your business, make sure that you are comfortable that they can take you with them on the path to growth and not leave you wondering what just happened.

No one can come into your business, wave a magic wand and make everything okay. A good freelancer, employee or consultant is one who doesn't just serve up what you asked for but rather exceeds your expectations. You should expect them to ask questions that make you think and challenge the way you do things. If you wanted everything to stay the same then you wouldn't be getting help. This resource can be the one that drives change and keeps everyone accountable.

The clearer you are about what you want and expect then the better chance you have of getting it.

SUMMARY

In determining what personnel are right for your situation you'll need to ask a series of questions, both of yourself and your business as well as the intended hires.

From your perspective, you will need to consider what your goals are and what would be better done internally rather than outsourcing.

In choosing the right candidates you'll need to consider their experience, any recommendations or feedback they have, recommendations from others, their ability to market themselves or their own services, and their motivation.

What to look for varies for each type of marketing help as do the right questions to ask.

KEY ACTIONS

❖ If you have some companies in mind that you're considering working with, review their sites based on the tips provided.

❖ Take a look at a few of the different outsourcing websites and look at the types of projects posted and the outsourcers bidding on them.

PART 3
EXTRAS

NEXT STEPS...

You made it! Thank you for taking the time to read *Get Smarter Marketing*. We've covered a lot on our journey together—you've learned the key elements of your marketing plan, including performing a situational analysis of your business, analyzing your target market, preparing your marketing collateral, reaching your target market and keeping track of it all. You've also discovered how to put your plan in place with various processes and tools as well as getting the help you need to handle implementation.

You also have access to a range of bonus resources that will help you take your marketing to the next level, which I've listed at the back of this book so you can easily reference them as required.

If it all seems a little overwhelming, take a step back and review the key actions at the back of each chapter, starting at Chapter 1. Either set aside time to address each of the key points raised, or focus on Chapters

10 and 11 and make getting the help you need a priority. The first task of the person or people you hire can be working their way through the key actions listed and pulling it all together into a plan that will work for your business.

Having gone through all the information, you now have a solid understanding of what's possible with marketing and the key considerations you need to take into account. This will help you make better decisions about marketing your business, which, in turn, will maximize your resources and improve your results.

Good luck!

ABOUT THE AUTHOR

Jill Brennan, a marketing consultant, mentor and the founder of Harbren Marketing, has over 20 years experience in the small business trenches. She has worked in, with and for small businesses.

Her articles on marketing have been published in the Sydney Morning Herald, The Age, MyBusiness Magazine and Australian Anthill.

Over the years Jill has worked with many small business owners that were overwhelmed by the complexity of marketing their products or service and frustrated by 'marketing types' that sold them what they had rather than what the business needed.

Jill realized there was a gap in the marketing for coaching and training to empower small businesses to develop there own internal marketing engine to fuel their growth.

This book is part of her strategy to bridge that gap. The other part is the development of other resources and programs specifically for small business.

Find out more about Jill and Harbren Marketing at harbren.com.

ACKNOWLEDGEMENTS

Thanks to my family and friends for their encouragement and support, and for believing that I had something worthwhile to say.

Thank you to my team of proof readers—Amanda Bigelow, Mary Jane Cormack, Callan McDonnell, Monique Mackellar and Cameron Mackellar—for taking the time to read through the chapters and offer your helpful suggestions and tips.

Thanks to my fellow KPIs for your tips, encouragement and suggestions on many aspects related to this book from the cover design to the concepts and content.

I'd also like to thank all the business owners and professionals that I've worked with over the years who have inspired many of the learnings contained in this book.

Thank you to my two beautiful boys—Jack and Ben—for being who you are. I'm honored to share life with you and get to know you more each day. You've both taught me more than you'll ever know.

And thank you to John for being my chief supporter and always encouraging me to do whatever I feel compelled to launch myself into. Your good humor and faith that I know what I'm doing, even when there is no evidence to support that view, is much appreciated. I love you more than I can say.

RESOURCES

CUSTOMER SERVICE AND RESEARCH

- **Customer Relationship Managers**—there are a number of CRM systems that can work well for small businesses. Salesforce is probably one of the better-known systems. Other options include AgileCRM, CapsuleCRM, Zoho, Maximizer and Dynamics CRM. Costs and functionality vary for each and it's worth working out what you need and then investigating a few options before making your choice.

- **Help desk**—If your business receives a lot of customer queries or needs to provide a help center then helpdesk software like Zendesk can make the management and delivery of this information much easier. Zendesk is a paid service based on the number of users who have access to the system. It is a better way to handle customer problems than emails or scrap paper, as there are built-in follow-up processes. It is also relatively easy to set up a knowledge base to reduce customer problems.

- **Online customer research**—Two free tools are Quantcast and Google AdPlanner, which allow you to enter demographic information, interests, market size and get a list of relevant sites, which can spark ideas for sites to approach about advertising.

COLLATERAL DEVELOPMENT

- **Blog scheduling**—Try the free 'Editorial Calendar' plugin for WordPress.
- **Content plan template**—visit my website harbren.com/content-template for links to a content plan template created in Excel that you can download for free.
- **Video editing**—Camtasia is a recording and editing package for videos. It's relatively easy to use and offers a thirty-day free trial so you can try it out. Another one that is good for screenshots is Screencast.
- **Video creation**—there are tools available online that can make creating videos easily without having to hire a video production company. Animoto and Biteable are two that have a free service with a watermarked logo. There is a small charge to get a logo free version.
- **Audio editing**—Audacity is an audio editing tool that can help to streamline your audio, remove background noise and cut the 'ahs', 'ums' and pauses so that your podcast sounds more streamlined.
- **Graphic Design**—Canva is an online tool that enables the creation of a variety of design-oriented collateral from business cards to social media graphics, brochures, presentations and many others. If you have a knack for design you can use it to create your own images or use it to create rough designs to visually brief your designer.
- **Software**—having the Adobe Creative Cloud provides access to a range of software that can be very useful for marketers depending on their level of skills in the design and technical areas. Photoshop is great for creating images, Indesign for creating printed collateral and Dreamweaver for creating web

pages. Having staff trained in these areas gives you a lot of flexibility in being able to quickly solve problems without the additional expense and delay of getting it done by third party suppliers.

- **Content writing**—There are a number of content writing services available like CrowdContent, TextBroker and BlogMutt. They can produce articles, blog posts and eBooks on demand or a set number for a monthly fee.

- **Interactive tools**—there are tools that can help create interactive tools like quizzes, training, polls and games. Proprofs is one company that does this, Google Forms and Gravity Forms are two others.

- **Headlines**—a service has been created called Headline Analyzer by Coschedule that provides feedback on what headlines to use on your content. It can also be used for product names, page titles and anything else that needs a headline.

MARKETING PLATFORMS

- **Third-party affiliates**—Clickbank and ShareaSale are two large affiliate networks.

- **Directories**—True Local, Yellow Pages are general directories. Other ones like TripAdvisor and UrbanSpoon are focused on specific interests.

- **Email marketing**—There are a number of different third-party providers you can pick from when choosing a service for email marketing and sending content like newsletters. MailChimp and InfusionSoft are well known but vary considerably in price and features.

- **Facebook**—This communication and sharing website has 936 million daily users (March 2015), 41% of whom are over 35 years. It's best for directly reaching consumers.

- **Pinterest**—This photo-sharing website has 72.8 million users (April 2015). 26% of these users have an income over $100k and 68% of them are female (February 2012), making this platform best for directly reaching female consumers.

- **Instagram**—This photo- and video-sharing website has 300 million active users (January 2015), 76% of whom are under 35 years old (June 2014). 68% of users are female.

- **YouTube**—YouTube has 1 billion visitors each month and over 4 billion videos viewed daily (April 2014). 78% of users are male (April 2015). It's best for reaching consumers and business professionals.

- **Twitter**—This online message and information service has 302 million active users (March 2015), 37% of whom are aged between 18-29 (January 2015). It's best for directly reaching consumers.

- **LinkedIn**—This business-oriented social networking service has 364 million users (June 2015), 61% of whom are aged between 30-64 years (January 2015). It's best for directly reaching personnel within a business.

MEASUREMENT AND OPTIMISATION

- **Website tracking**—Google provides free website reporting through Google Analytics. The reporting available is comprehensive and allows users to drill into a variety of areas including visitor demographics, how visitors flow through your website, where they are located, what browser they're using, what percentage are using a tablet or mobile to reach your site.

- **Email tracking**—Most third-party email providers will offer tracking of your emails' open and click-through rates.

- **Social media tracking**—Hootsuite offers tracking for posts scheduled within its platform, while some social media platforms like Facebook have in-built tracking for business pages.
- **Customer surveys**—Survey Monkey and Survey Gizmo are two affordable online survey services. Both charge a monthly fee for ongoing access.
- **Website functionality**—a slow loading website is frustrating for everyone. Google has a range of tools that can help you see how they view your site. One that is very useful is called PageSpeed. It assesses how fast your page loads both on desktop and mobile and flags potential problems. Knowing this information can help you better brief a developer and focus on those areas that are going to have the biggest impact on performance.
- **SEO Analysis**—there are a lot of different tools available to assess how usable and findable your site is. Some that you can experiment with are Website Grader from Hubspot, SEO Report Card from Upcity and Site Analyzer.

FINDING MARKETING HELP

- **Freelancers**—You can source freelancers on Upwork and Freelancer. For small jobs, Fiverr connects you with freelancers prepared to do specific tasks from $5. 99designs is a graphic design freelancing website which works like an online design competition. You only pay if you find and select a winner.

WORKING OUT YOUR BIG PICTURE

- **Books**—*The Values Factor* by John Demartini and *Start with Why* by Simon Sinek are books that you can read if you want to explore this area more deeply.
- **Videos**—a more concise way to access Simon Sinek is through his TED talks. He has done several talks now but 'Start With

Why' is the one that led to his book. You will get the main points in 18 minutes and can then decide if you need to learn more.

With any resources, things change over time. For an up-to-date resources list visit harbren.com/resources.

Morgan James
Speakers Group

www.TheMorganJamesSpeakersGroup.com

We connect Morgan James published authors with live and online events and audiences whom will benefit from their expertise.